Other Books by Cathay O. Reta

Keep Walking, Your Heart Will Catch Up:

A Camino de Santiago Journey

Joy Unfolding: Messages for the Guarded Heart

Praise for Dance in the Meadow

"I like this book. Cathay is authentic in what she shares and every time someone is authentic, they're helping someone else overcome their fears and shame for having felt the same way. I also like the casualness of it . . . It's the way I talk with God." –Jack Canfield, co-author of the bestselling *Chicken Soup for the Soul* series and a pioneer in the field of Personal Development and Peak Performance

"Cathay is so thought-provoking while also being hopeful. This is what true self-awareness and enlightenment look like. Humanity is longing for inspiration like this." –Katharyn O. Muniz, Chief Executive Officer, Orange County Conservation Corps

"I love this book! Cathay draws you into her world, conversing with the reader like you would an old friend. She shares her path out of a 'religion' gone wrong into a personal journey of communing with God. It gives the reader permission to question why you believe what you believe while bringing you into deeper understanding and leading you to do some soul-searching of your own. I give *Dance in the Meadow* my greatest endorsement." –Kim Sorrelle, author of best-sellers including *Love Is*

Dance In The Meadow

Conversations of Self-Discovery, Clarity, and Love

Cathay O. Reta

Keep Walking Publications

Dance in the Meadow

© 2023 Cathay O. Reta

Keep Walking Publications. All rights reserved.

Printed in Spokane Valley, Washington

Scripture quotations are taken from The Holy Bible, English Standard Version® (ESV®). Copyright © 2001 by Crossway, a publishing ministry of Good News Publishers. All rights reserved.

Book Cover: BookCoverZone

Paperback ISBN: 979-8-9881172-0-9

E-book ISBN: 979-8-9881172-1-6

Cataloging-in-Publication Data is available from the Library of Congress.

To Kathleen

Thank you for a calm space in which to meditate and to pray, for inspiring conversations and insightful thoughts, and for laughter and tears.

Whenever we're led out of normalcy into sacred, open space, it's going to feel like suffering, because it is letting go of what we're used to. This is always painful at some level. But part of us has to die if we are ever to grow larger (John 12:24). If we're not willing to let go and die to our small, false self, we won't enter into any new or sacred space.

—Father Richard Rohr,
   "Order, Disorder, Reorder"[1]

Contents

Dance in the Meadow   13
Preface   15

PART I
Beginning   23

1. The Start of It All   25
2. Step Away from the Woods   28
3. I'm Watching You   32
4. In a Little While   35
5. A Walk in the Rain   37
6. Do You Trust Me?   40
7. Hidden Treasure   42

PART II
Tilling the Ground   45

8. The Filters   47
9. Breathing Deeply   49
10. Hope Pulled Off a Shelf   52
11. The Secret Garden   55
12. For Singing Out Loud   58
13. Alive and Blessed to Be Alive   60
14. No Baby   62

PART III
Growing Roots   67

15. Everybody Loves Cathay   69
16. The Reluctant Pioneer   72
17. The Mountain Before Me   75
18. The Refreshing   77
19. Learning to Believe   79
20. Rolling with God   81
21. The Line of Scrimmage   83

PART IV
Blooming   87

22. Push Harder   89
23. Riding in the Canoe   92
24. Climbing the Mountain   94
25. Live Life   97
26. Freedom   99
27. Take Out the Trash   101
28. Turn Around and Look   104

PART V
Pruning   107

29. Bowels of Mercy   109
30. Let Your Heart Break   112
31. Be Still   114
32. Just Be   116
33. No Do-Overs   118
34. Aerate the Soul   121
35. Fly Like an Eagle—Really?   123

PART VI
Becoming   127

36. Numbness   129
37. Let's Talk About Love   131
38. To Receive Love   133
39. From the Core of Your Being   137
40. Jump into the Deep End   139
41. They're Just Like Me   142

Conclusion   147
Notes   149
Acknowledgments   151
About the Author   153

Dance in the Meadow

Preface

My story, this book, is a testament to what Franciscan priest Richard Rohr describes as the "wisdom pattern."[1] My journey into sacredness takes place during a time of upheaval in my life. A time of letting go. A time of pain. A time of searching. And a time of growing.

I believe it can help others wrestle the truth of their being from the clutches of the façades we create to hide away that which we deem unacceptable. The façades that conform to what society expects of us, that conform to what we expect of ourselves. These façades are our face of order, where we have meticulously labeled every thought, every action, every belief, and set each carefully in its place. Neat and orderly. Black and white. We rest feeling that we are in control, all is well. We know what's right and what's wrong.

Then there comes a time of chaos—of disorder. A time when we are forced, or at least, given the option, to review what we have labeled as truth about who we are and how we fit into the universe. Only then, only when we can embrace chaos and reconsider what is true, can we reorder our lives and emerge stronger and with greater clarity. Then we can turn our gazes inside and find our true selves no longer cowering in a corner, pretending to disappear. Then we can see our truth with gentle acceptance and life-giving grace.

When I began to document my conversations with God, I never intended to share them in a book. They were personal. They sustained me and taught me. They informed my understanding of my spiritual journey. However, as I shared bits and pieces of these writings with others, I found that my journey is not unique. Many are traveling over the same terrain I have covered. Many people struggle to find their place in life, their identity. They seek to uncover the sense of self that they have lost somewhere along life's pathway. This book is for them.

These particular conversations started one year after David, my husband of thirty-three years, passed away. David was a pastor and evangelist with an international Christian ministry. I worked alongside him. We were a well-fit team, complementing each other with our strengths and talents and consoling each other in our weaknesses. We counseled couples through marital troubles, spiritual struggles, addictions, and times of doubt. We prayed with and laid hands on the sick for their recovery. We experienced miracles. We spoke in tongues, and we prophesied. We encouraged individuals who came to us looking for reassurance and direction. We walked alongside hundreds of people in their spiritual growth.

We traveled together in ministry even after David experienced renal failure. He went on peritoneal dialysis, a treatment he would perform daily at home or from whatever home or hotel room we were in as we traveled. We were proud that his dialysis did not deter us from our ministry activities. He thrived. We felt we could overcome anything. And we did overcome every challenge that came our way.

David's first stroke changed that. It ushered in a time of shaking. Yet, looking back, I am acutely aware that our shaking had already begun long before the stroke. In the previous half-dozen years, we had questioned some events and behaviors we had seen within our ministry group. We were troubled by some of the teachings shared. In the spirit of submission, we would sometimes voice our concerns about these things, but we mostly kept our doubts to ourselves.

In addition to ministry work, I had been active in the field of adult literacy for the past forty years. I worked on a local level, managing programs in public libraries. I had also worked on the state and national levels. As a consultant to a few organizations, I designed and facilitated workshops around the country. As I grew discontent with the ministry, I slowly began to focus more on this area of my life and less on that of the ministry. I compartmentalized my life. Literacy work in one place, spiritual matters in another.

David's first stroke was followed by a heart attack the next month, a second stroke the third month, and then an ongoing string of small strokes. Over the following four years until his death, we were pulled and pushed, uplifted and downcast, filled with hope and then discouraged. My foundation unraveled. I now questioned what I had once been so sure of, but I lacked the energy to respond to my doubts and to search for answers. David and I drifted. I drifted into numbness, into the role of caregiver. David ultimately drifted into death. I girded myself with all the faith I could muster to continue without him.

I had no children. I was alone. A dear family that was part of the ministry invited me to live with them in Indiana, and I felt a tug in my heart confirming that this was what I needed. So, I retired from my literacy job, left Los Angeles, and found a new home in rural Indiana with this family.

Two months after arriving at my new home, I left the ministry I had been growing discontent with. I'd grown up in this ministry. I'd been a part of it from its inception in 1972, when the founder and his wife first began gatherings in their home. I had traveled with them throughout the United States and Mexico as part of the ministry team. When I married David in 1983, my involvement continued in the role of pastor's wife.

Now, more than forty-five years later, I felt that the group, its practices and doctrines, had steered far off course. We proclaimed that we were the only ones with the truth. We had developed a lot of erroneous thinking. I could no longer support the beliefs and continue in them. I wasn't the only one who came to that decision. The family I lived with and about half of the church group also left.

I began to reconsider everything I had believed and face the doubts I previously ignored. My faulty foundation was breaking up. I turned from the façade I had worn for so long and questioned my true identity. I sought greater meaning in life. It was a time of discovery and learning and restoration.

My Indiana home was the perfect setting for this season of time. I settled into the top floor of the three-story house situated in the middle of eighty acres, surrounded by meadows, woods, and the family's horses. It was like a retreat with amenities including a heated swimming pool in the backyard, weightlifting equipment, a treadmill, a stationary bike, an oxygen treatment apparatus in the basement, and a dry sauna on the main floor. My friend and host Kathleen, a naturopathic doctor, treated me with energy medicine, biofeedback sessions, herbal remedies, and other modalities that I never understood but appreciated. She and I spent many mornings talking, laughing, crying, and processing what was happening in this spiritual shaking—or, rather, awakening.

My first conversation took place when I stepped into the dry sauna one day. It unfolded in my mind like a vision. I wrote it down after I stepped out of the sauna and returned to my room. That became a pattern for me when I would go into the sauna. I'd have a conversation and write it down afterward. Then the conversations overflowed from my sauna time to other physical spaces—seated in the recliner beside my bedroom window, walking around a nearby lake, or simply sitting outside.

People often ask me how is it that I hear God's voice. Is it audible? No. I hear his voice in my mind the same way I hear my own voice when I'm thinking. The words come from my heart, from my core, from my center. It is that voice . . . that still, small, inner voice.

I've learned to trust that voice and, by faith, recognize it as God. I ask, he answers. I've experienced it many times over, and now it is a common experience for me. But certainly, while it is common, it is not anything I take for granted. I am as appreciative of it now as I was the first time I heard this voice from inside me.

When I began having this series of conversations, the experience was uplifting and insightful. It was fun, like getting to know a new lover; teasing, smiling, and laughing together. It provided an opportunity for deep reflection, sharing thoughts and forming ideas previously unspoken. I was sometimes quite surprised by what poured out on the page. I learned to trust God even more.

For a year I regularly engaged in these conversations and then documented them on my laptop. It was intense spiritual therapy. I continue to converse with God, but not as intensely as I did during this time of healing and restoration.

Perhaps this season was foretold in a song that I wrote a few years before my life began to unravel. Perhaps my Lord was calling to me then, preparing me for what lay ahead. He called me to a meadow. A meadow I began to see in visions during this year of conversations with him.

My hope is that my private and personal conversations with God will inspire you. I hope they will spark truth within you and motivate you to uncover your own songs and stories. I hope you will gain insight and confidence to trust your inner voice. I hope you will find and appreciate the treasure that you are.

If you would like to share your stories, I would love to hear them. I would love to know how our life experiences repeat and intersect and support each other's.

You can contact me through my website: www.cathayreta.com

Dance in the Meadow
words and music by Cathay Reta

Softly he comes to me, whispering my name
In the morning, at first break of day
Saying, open your eyes my beloved, my fair one
Come dance in the meadow with me

Dance in the meadow
Come dance with abandon
With hands lifted up, let your spirit fly free
Rejoice in a new song, my love song unto you
Come dance in the meadow with me

Softly he comes to me, taking my hand
In the stillness he whispers my name
Saying, rise up my fair one, a full moon is rising
Come dance in the moonlight with me

Dance in the moonlight and join with the stars
As they cast a new glow on the sky up above
Come sway to the music, let my love surround you
Come dance in the moonlight with me

Softly he beckons, his voice calling gently
He whispers my name once again
Saying, I am the one you have looked for, have longed for

Come dance forever with me

Dance on the streets paved with gold, lined with precious
    jewels
    Listen to voices of angels rejoice
    Rise up, my fair one, your name I am calling
    Come dance in the heavens with me

You can listen to Dance in the Meadow here: https://www.
cathayreta.com/may-i-have-this-dance/

Part One

Beginning

Chapter 1

The Start of It All

I walk a twenty-six-minute mile on the treadmill this afternoon. That's slow. I know. I'm just beginning to work out my body after years of sitting at a desk throughout most of the day. I've begun a regimen of walking to get my body moving, but today it's too cold to walk outside. I'm not quite used to the frigid temperatures of late fall in my new Indiana home. I've lived most of my life in warm climates—Phoenix and then Los Angeles. I'm slowly adapting to the cold, but today I've opted to walk on the treadmill in the basement.

I've decided to establish a routine of following my walks with a session in the dry sauna. I look forward to the benefit of sweating out toxins while I relax. What bliss! I tell the Lord I'll use the sauna time for worship and communion with him. Then I strip down, click on Eric Clapton on my iPhone, and turn up the music loud enough to hear it just outside the door. I step into the wood box, which is now 108 degrees and climbing.

"I thought this was our time together," the Lord says to me. "What's with Eric Clapton?"

"Oh! Sorry," I respond as I step out and turn off the music.

"Don't know what I was thinking. But yes, Lord, I want to talk with you about—"

"Why do you always have to talk first?" he interrupts. "Why don't you let me start the conversation?"

Silence.

"Okay. You go, Lord." I know it's a moment to be quiet. But after a few minutes, I say, "Lord . . ." and he hushes me before I can continue.

More silence.

"What about—"

"Tsch," he says, the same way dog whisperer Cesar Millan talks to dogs when he wants them to display a *calm, submissive* attitude. Okay, I get it, and I'm quiet as far as talking to the Lord. But my mind wanders to talk with other people—people who aren't even here!

When I'm finally able to pull out of those imaginations, the Lord shows me a brief glimpse of a special place. A peaceful meadow. Its colors are soft and alluring. Tall grass moves gently with the breeze, dancing under a warm sun. I want to hang out there. I want to lie on the ground and feel nature cradle my body.

"No," the Lord tells me. "You're not ready. Not today." He can't trust me with that yet because I only want to have the experience so I can then go around and tell everyone about it. I want to brag about how wonderful it is. I can't simply let it be.

I'm reminded of when my father was teaching me how to drive. One day we were driving down our little neighborhood street, and I saw a couple of friends walking nearby. I waved out the window to them in a way that said, "Hey, look at me! I'm driving!"

"Stop that!" my dad barked. "You just pay attention to the road. Forget about who's out there."

I think God is saying that's the concern he has about me just hanging out in the meadow. And sadly, I get it. I know

I'm not ready . . . yet. I pull my thoughts back to God. He begins to draw me into the silence again, but I go on a mental walk around the neighborhood, thinking about this and that and what I need to do today.

"You see what I'm working with?" God asks.

"Yes. Why do I do that?"

"It's that concern you have about what others think of you. It's like a sheath that covers you. You're never satisfied to just be you, you alone, you alone with me. But that'll change. That sheath is peeling away. Little sister . . ."

Suddenly my mind turns the station, and I'm hearing Elvis sing "Little Sister," a song he made famous in the 1960s. It's about girls who kiss, say it's nice, and then run. Is the Lord comparing me to them?

"Oh! Sorry! I'm back, Lord," I reassure him. Then I start to think about what fun it will be to write about this conversation with God.

"Shouldn't you have the conversation first?" he interrupts.

"Oh, right. I'm all yours. I'll try."

And I do try but can never fully get into the place of silence where there is true worship and nothing else. Then the sauna timer turns off. My twenty minutes are up. *Maybe I can just sit here a little longer and enter into meditation,* I think. But I know that isn't to be.

I've been given what I can receive for today, and I know the sheath is peeling off to unveil more. All will come forth in time.

Chapter 2

Step Away from the Woods

I get in a brief workout on my arms today—brief because I experience muscle cramps in my right arm after only two minutes on the weight machines. *¡Ay, chihuahua!* I move to the treadmill and twenty-five minutes later into the dry sauna. The sauna is turning out to be my best time to visit with the Lord.

I place my towel on the warm wooden bench and take a seat. I welcome my time with the Lord. In a vision I see him sitting on top of a picnic table across an open meadow. I walk over and sit beside him. He says nothing. I say nothing. After a while I begin to squirm and become restless. He puts his arm around me and pulls me close. I cry and share that I really just want to go and sit in the forest behind us. Where I can see out but no one can see me.

"That's pretty much how I roll," I say.

"No," he says and continues to hold me close. I cry. I cry for no reason and for every reason all at once—for everything that has hurt. Every sadness, every tiredness. I cry in relief and appreciation for his tight hug, his comforting touch.

"I just want to cry."

"Then cry," he tells me. "It's okay. You've held in too

much. You've hidden so much away that you don't even know why you cry. I know why. And I know you've padded your body with fat to cover that which you don't want to see. To cover the hurt."

"Lord, I think that's a little rude. I'm embarrassed at the turn this is taking."

"It's your conversation." He laughs. "I didn't set this up. You did."

"Well, I'd rather hide in the woods." I sense that, in a very real way, what I'm doing to my body is impacting my soul, and what is happening in my soul is impacting my body. I'm beginning to lose some of the fat that I've evidently hidden myself with. My new activity of walking is starting to have some effect; and I sense that when more fat is cleared away, I will see and understand what it has covered. This is a self-discovery type of mojo.

It makes me think of my new pair of Vera Bradley designer glasses. The outside of the frames is plain black. But the inside—the part no one can see but me—is a pretty turquoise blue in the front with a paisley design on the sides. As I looked at them the other day, I thought, *That's me.* Plain on the outside but colorful inside. I do feel like the true me is a lively and colorful person. But I don't show that. On the outside I've learned to conform to expectations of what I'm supposed to do or not do. To put on a facade.

I'm no longer comfortable living like that. I would like my outward persona to move over and make room for what's inside. I'd like to find the real me and release her into the world.

And so I sit at the table and cry.

"It's okay," the Lord reassures me. "You don't have to break through and get everything out all at once. It's a process. A process for you, anyway. I'm already at the end—I know the results. And I know that one day you will step away from the woods. You will dance freely in this meadow, with abandon and without care.

"Meanwhile, don't worry about the process, but don't neglect it either. Cry today, and we'll talk more tomorrow."

"Okay. Tomorrow."

* * *

I can't seem to let go of what's bothering me, of why I want to hide in the woods and not be seen. Then I start to remember a couple of the very few memories I have from childhood. I guess I've always been given to hiding. I was shy and embarrassed to be seen. When my brother was in first grade and I was about four years old, he made a friend at school. He said he was going to bring him home to meet me the next day. I didn't want to meet anyone. So that next day when I knew he would be coming in from school, I hid.

I crawled under my parents' bed. I lay there awhile until it occurred to me that was the first place my brother would look. So I slipped out from under the bed and moved to my mother's closet. I closed the door and pushed my way into the back corner, behind her clothes hanging down. There I sat in darkness.

Sure enough, before long I could hear that Larry was home. And sure enough, the closet door soon opened. "That's my sister, Cathay," he said to his friend, pointing at me. Then they turned and left. I don't know how long I stayed in the closet, but I think it was a long time. I was extremely embarrassed and didn't know what to do next.

I also remember hiding in the kitchen cabinet when my father came home from work. I'd always thought of this as playing hide-and-seek. Then one day I watched an old 8-mm video clip of my father walking up the sidewalk, coming home from work. A heavy equipment operator, he was covered with dirt and carrying his lunch box.

Look at that mean man! The thought escaped my mind before I could catch myself, before I could censor myself. Suddenly, I realized that what I had remembered as a game of hide-and-seek with my father was not a game at all. I had been afraid of him.

My dad struggled with alcoholism in my earliest years. Then he came to the Lord and began going to church. After that he never drank again. I was about eight years old when that dynamic changed our family.

I recall one night a few years after he and my mom began going to church with me. My dad gave his testimony at a special service and shared that he used to have a problem with alcohol. He told the congregation about a particular night when he came home drunk. As he neared the door, inside he could hear my brother and me begging Mom to lock him out. I have no memory of that. I also don't remember much of why I would have begged her to lock him out. Yet as I reflect on this, I do catch glimpses of situations in which the effects of alcoholism clearly disrupted our household. I think my way of dealing with the disruption was to hide and forget what I had seen. Clearly, there's a pattern here. I have learned to deal with life's struggles by hiding.

Yes, I've covered over a lot. I've pressed down so much—put it out of my memory. I've watched life from the woods rather than sitting in the middle of it. Rather than living it.

I ask the Lord what to do about it.

"You don't have to break through and get everything out all at once," he assures me. "It's a process."

I hold on to the words he said to me, to stay away from the woods. Hmm . . . *Step away from the woods.* Yes, a new mantra for me.

Step away from the woods.

Chapter 3

I'm Watching You

"I'm watching you," the Lord says when I step into the sauna and get ready for our time together. In my vision I see him low to the ground, squatting, sitting on his heels the way my Vietnamese friend used to do. That posture has always amazed me. I admire such ability since I cannot balance myself like that at all. I have to hold on to something or I'll fall over sideways. But here's the Lord, comfortably squatting beside the picnic bench where we usually sit and talk.

"I'm just watching you," he says again.

"That can't be very exciting," I say. We're silent for a bit, and I'm uncomfortable. "Why would you want to just watch me?" I ask.

"You're beautiful."

That makes me even more uncomfortable. It takes me back to age nine when my brother and I were playing hide-and-seek with a couple of friends while all our parents visited. A new family was there, too, along with their son, whom I'd met only that night. At one point as we all came out from hiding, the new kid walked toward me and called, "Hey, beautiful." I kicked him. I kicked him in the shin and ran. I didn't know how to respond to that word. I still don't. Fortunately for the Lord, I no longer kick and run, but being called *beautiful* makes me flinch.

The Lord continues. "It's like what parents feel as they watch their children. They sit and just watch in awe and wonder at how their kids are growing, learning, and developing. I get joy from watching you."

I'm ready to point out that I have no children so I don't know what he's talking about. Then I remember I have experienced a bit of what he's describing. I do understand.

The Chesleys opened their family to me when I was in my early twenties. I spent a lot of time with John and Irma and their four children at their home in the small Arizona town of Valley Farms. I recall an occasion when I was in awe and filled with laughter to witness their youngest developing his personality.

When Jonathan was maybe two years old, his mother and I were seated at the kitchen table and talking. He handed his cup to me and said, "Mama." The glimmer in his eye made it very clear that he was telling a joke by referring to me as his mother. I've always cherished this wondrous moment—when I watched Jonathan begin to embrace humor. So precious.

On another occasion a few years later, I watched as Jonathan's father was disciplining him. I don't recall what Jonathan had done, but his father, understanding how best to relate to children, lowered himself to his knees so he could talk to his son eye to eye and not tower above him. He explained why what he'd done was wrong.

Out of nowhere, little Jonathan formed a fist and popped his dad in the nose. Straight on. Perfect shot. I hurt from holding in my laughter. It was rather fun to watch, to see how children develop. What goes through their minds? How do they put information together and come up with such reactions?

I don't know that this is the kind of watching my Lord is

enjoying, but I return my attention to him. We take a seat at the table. I'm glad for that because I don't want to squat on the ground with him. I know he loves me and is proud of me. I sense that nothing I could do would make him turn away from me or be angry. Yes, he loves me, and he likes to watch me grow and learn and develop into the person he knows is in me.

I appreciate that. I think I'll let it settle in and permeate my soul. I'll humble myself and let myself be called beautiful. I'll accept the love and attention my Lord is giving me.

He's watching me, and it's a good thing.

Chapter 4

In a Little While

"In a little while you will see," the Lord says to me this morning. "You will see when it is time to see."

Sitting in the chair beside my third-story window, I look out at an unusual happening. The leaves are turning and dropping off the red maple tree just a few feet away. That in and of itself is not unusual. What's unusual is that this is happening in late January. The tree normally would have done this months ago, but it did not. It didn't follow the timetable set for the seasons, even though those tables are based on observance of what happens in nature.

This year the weather changed. The cold delayed its arrival. And so the leaves stayed a bit longer. Now they are beginning to turn and drop.

"I can't go by what I've seen in the past. Is that it, Lord?" I ask while feeling the question is both trivial and trite. Of course that's the case. I've learned a little something about that, but I know there must be more. I need to dig deeper.

"What is it I'm not seeing, Lord? What am I missing here?"

"You're missing nothing," he responds. "Everything happens when it is time to happen. Not because of a calendar date, not because of wishing it so, not because someone tells you it is time. It happens when it is ready, just as nature matures and changes one season to the next because the earth and the atmosphere have been prepped. They conspire, and they call the change forth."

"All working in harmony," I say.

As I reflect, I get the sense that my journey into meditation and learning to be still has much to do with letting nature unfold in its time. My life will unfold when my soul and spirit—like the earth and the atmosphere—have been prepped and call it forth. Whether the action is to blaze a trail or simply relax in a warm stream, everything has its time.

"Yes, that's right," the Lord says. "Your life will unfold when it is time—day by day, moment by moment. Just as the trees don't withhold nutrition and push their leaves off simply because tradition says they should, neither does your life flow in response to some timeline developed and practiced by those who have gone before you.

"Not now. Not today. Relax and allow life to unfold in its time, in its purpose. One day you will look back and see the gentle unfolding that has come forth. You'll find yourself already where you never imagined you could be."

It occurs to me that we may be talking about climbing a mountain. I've had glimpses of it looming in front of me. I know I will climb it one day, just not today. There's nothing to fret. Nothing to fear. When it's time I will be ready. But not now. Not today.

Chapter 5

A Walk in the Rain

The rain! How beautiful! How refreshing! And mesmerizing! As it begins to rain today, I recall my youth when I loved to walk and run in the rain. It was so much fun. Getting wet felt good. So why did that change when I became an adult?

I go outside and walk around awhile, disappointed that the rain has turned out to be just a simple drizzle. *But it's a good start,* I think. I walk across the green lawn, down the driveway and out toward the pastures, down to the horse arena and back. My Indiana home offers a good mix of terrain to explore and allows me to appreciate nature's diversity. Slowly the drops pick up to a steady light rain. So lovely. Feeling the coolness on my face, I think about watching myself walk in the rain.

"When did I stop living my life and become a spectator, a commentator about my life?" I ask. A new perspective is suddenly obvious. I'm an outside observer. Maybe I'm just like the Lord squatting beside the picnic table and watching me. But it's not my place to be watching life go by, hidden in the woods. I want to be living inside it.

I talk with the Lord about it and determine I will, from

this day on, be involved. I will participate in my life and no longer sit on the sidelines watching it from a distance. I know it will be challenging to keep that focus and not continually drift into an observer role. Still, that is my resolve.

"Lord, make it rain harder," I plead. "Rain on me. I want to feel every bit of it. I want the waters to wash over me and awaken every sense in my being." It doesn't rain any harder, but I begin to feel an awakening. I feel so alive.

"Lord, what are these emotions? These stirrings inside me?"

"It's my spirit. It's your spirit," he tells me. "That is the spirit leading and guiding you and loving you. Embrace it and nurture it." Steadily growing wetter, I look into the sky and appreciate the darkness of the clouds and the bounty they release.

"Why is it that we have learned to run inside—out of the rain?" I ask. "It's your creation. It's beautiful, and it has purpose. Why are we so compelled to hide from it?"

"Man has strange ways," the Lord says. "He is fearful, and he runs. He assigns labels of *good* and *bad* to everything around him, never stopping to talk with me about it. He never takes time to be still and listen. He labels something as bad, and then he runs away from it.

"I'm pleased you have chosen not to run any longer. I'm pleased you have chosen to explore the garden I made for you. I'm pleased when you stop and appreciate the life all around you. When you let it nurture your soul. That is a beginning to healing. That is why today you can run into the rain instead of running away from it."

"Teach me, Lord. Teach me to love you by loving what you have made. Show me how to look, how to see what is life before me and to know what is life in me."

I sit on the bench under the red maple tree and stay awhile. The rain is slow and light now. "I want to get drenched, Lord! Send a torrential rain!"

Nothing.

"Please, Lord. Make it rain harder. I want to be drenched."

"Of course, you do," he says, "because then you can check it off your list—'I walked in the rain; I got drenched.' And then you will go inside and go about your business looking for something else. You will forget all about this experience. A heavy rain would not serve you well right now."

I understand. I recognize myself in what he is saying.

"I know how to woo you, my precious one. Take in this light rain today, and on another day we'll walk in the rain again and again and again. You will come to know me deeper and deeper, and yes, you will be soaked, drenched. But it will be through the steady flow, a process of getting to know each other, and it will be good."

"Thank you, Lord. I get it." I continue to sit on the bench. I have a new appreciation for these mystical drops that fall from the sky.

Chapter 6

Do You Trust Me?

C athay, do you trust me?" the Lord asks, calling me by name as I sit staring out the window.

"No, not today," I respond. "Today I'm afraid."

I'm reminded of my hesitation when driving along a road that goes up a hill so steep I can't see what's on the other side until I reach the top. It fills me with dread. I'm never quite sure I won't see a car coming at me in my lane or some blockage in the road. Or maybe the road will just not be there.

Blind spots do not sit well with me.

I feel like that's where I am today. I feel like I'm in a blind spot.

It's been two years since David died. A year since moving to Indiana. I'm feeling like I would like to know what will happen with me at this juncture. I'm a widow now, after thirty-three years of marriage. What's next? Where will my life take me? Yet, at the same time, I know it's not a good idea for me to know. If I knew, I would likely sidestep the issues I need to work out in my heart. I recall the line from *A Few Good Men*. Jack Nicholson is shouting out, "The truth? You can't handle the truth!"[1]

I smile and then listen to the Lord.

"I am the truth," he says. "To know me is to know truth, and I would have you to know me completely. Intimately, with no separation between us. Your emotions that make you want to know the future are just emotions. They press. They distract. They are prompted by fear and push away trust."

"I kind of get it, Lord. I have a sense that deep within, I do fear truth."

"Yes, you fear what you don't know in completeness. Those fears produce the emotions that pull you away. They make you shy away from trusting me.

"Stand still, and let truth come to you. Let it cover you and hold you firm. Do not seek truth. Don't go running after a perception that will only take you down a dark alley. Rather, stand and rest in your being, in oneness with me, as much as you understand it now. That's enough for now."

"I hear you, Lord. I put too much thinking into this. My mind is doing what it is so trained to do—to strategize. To think through the details, to anticipate what scenarios may happen so I can be prepared for them. So very busy, all based on what might be . . . not trusting what is. Not trusting I'll be ready for tomorrow when it comes."

"That's right," the Lord says. "Just take care of today. That will prepare you for tomorrow."

I close my eyes, walking without regard to where I'm going, why I'm going there, or what lays ahead for me. Just walking. Just talking with God. Just being.

"Yes, I trust you, Lord. Fully. Totally. You have proven yourself to me time and time again. I trust you and know that wherever we walk, you've got me. It's safe, and it is good."

"That's all I ask today. That's all," he says.

Chapter 7

Hidden Treasure

In today's vision I sit at the picnic bench alone, my eyes cast to the ground. Then I hear his voice. My Lord is behind me.

"The ground won't change just by you looking at it," he teases. "You will need to get off the bench and work it. What you put into it is what you will get out of it. Go ahead. Break up the ground. Bring the soft soil to the top, and then let's look at what to plant."

"What if, after turning the soil over, I leave it to just grow what is in it. I'm not so sure I need to plant new seed, Lord."

"You've certainly done enough planting throughout your lifetime," he says. "There is quite a mix of what lays in the dirt."

"I think it's time to let that come out, let it grow, then see what to do after that. I don't see a need to throw anything new into the ground right now."

"You have spoken well," the Lord tells me. "You have spoken well, and that's what we will do."

We sit on the ground and break up the dry earth, revealing the fresh, cool dirt that was stuck under the dry top layer. We take a break and let the soil sit as we stretch out on the ground, eyes upward to the sky. I drift to sleep, thinking, *What will show up? What is in the ground?*

"Hidden treasures," the Lord says, answering the questions on my heart once I wake up. "You have planted and stored so much. Now let it produce fruit. Let its life force come out to give you the nourishment you need to finish out this day, this period of time. I'll wait with you."

It strikes me that the ambiguity of this conversation gives me comfort. So often, I want to know the specifics. I demand to know the answers. But not knowing everything has its place, too, and right now I'm comfortable with it.

"Ah," I say to the Lord. "This is why we aren't planting anything new. All that I am for this phase of life is already in the ground, already within me. It is merely waiting for the strength to break through its shell and poke its way to the sky."

"Yes. So it is, my daughter. I will wait with you, and then together we will assess the garden and decide what to do next."

Part Two

Tilling the Ground

Chapter 8

The Filters

It's another day in the sauna, sweating out the old toxins and taking in new meditations with the Lord. Today in the spirit I see myself stumble into the garden where the Lord is sitting. "I can't seem to walk straight." I laugh. "I'm walking like I'm drunk."

"Yes, I noticed you were staggering like a drunkard. Anything you want to tell me?"

"No, I'm not drunk. Really."

"I know," he responds, "but the truth is, some people are only able to speak what's on their heart, what's close and dear to them, when they are drunk."

I'm sixty-three years old and have never been drunk. That's because of my church upbringing and expectations. I used to tell my husband David that I'd like to get drunk, that I would like to see what it would be like. I could picture myself as being fun and laughing and having a good time. But David assured me I'd probably be one of those drunks who cry in their beer. Not a pretty sight. Not any fun to be around. He's probably right.

"If you like, we can have our conversation and you can act

as if you're drunk," the Lord says. "If you need that to get past your filters and speak what's on your heart, I'm down."

I consider the invitation.

"Or," he continues, "I can help you lift those filters."

Lifting the filters seems like a better option. I feel the Lord's tenderness. I know he will help me reveal myself little by little, protecting me as I become more comfortable. I'm confident that he would not use shock treatment. He wouldn't rip open the shower curtain and leave me suddenly naked and exposed for all the world to see. I know that he will work patiently.

I do want to be authentic—the same on the outside as on the inside. Not hiding or covering any secrets. A *what-you-see-is-what-you-get* kind of girl. Free.

"Okay, let's do it," I tell him. "Let's lift those filters." And thus continues my journey into authenticity.

Chapter 9

Breathing Deeply

Sauna time, and the visions come streaming . . . (*Sung to the tune of "Summertime."*)

I walk cheerfully to our picnic bench in the meadow and greet the Lord.

"Take a deep breath. Let it fill you," he tells me.

I do. I take a couple of them, using my diaphragm to take air deep into my midsection. I slowly inhale, slowly exhale. "That feels so good," I say, taking one more.

"That's what it feels like to breathe freely, with your whole body," he says.

I suddenly sense where this is going. "You mean instead of breathing shallowly while simultaneously sucking in your gut and trying to look . . . less fat?"

I've long since gotten past trying to look *skinny*. That has never been in the realm of possibilities. Now, just looking *a little less fat* is my goal. You know how it is. Well, maybe you know. It's like when someone is taking your picture and you want to look good, you straighten up, bring your shoulders back, and suck in your gut. Trouble is, I've found myself trying to walk around like that—all the time. I can barely breathe.

"Right," the Lord chimes back in. "You're hurting your body. You're squeezing and twisting your insides and no longer taking in full breaths. And you don't even realize it."

"True."

"It is damaging."

I have this mental picture of my cells and all their little members trying to do their work. They try to get through the vessel doorways to bring in nutrients, to pump in oxygen, to draw out toxins. But too often, the cells get stuck. They try and try, but I've contorted my body in such a way that some doors are bent at an extreme angle. They will not pry open. They're damaged.

"The same thing happens in your soul," the Lord says. "You *suck it up*, acting like things don't bother you when they do. You try to look less angry, less hurt. Your lies are killing you. They're not letting life flow freely through you. And just like when you don't even realize you're holding your breath or sucking in your stomach (and feeling uncomfortable and hurting your insides) . . . sometimes you don't even know when your feelings are hurt or when something bothers you."

"Oh." It's true. I'm gradually becoming aware of that.

"But we're working on that," the Lord says.

* * *

Leaving this vision aside, I'm reminded of when the Lord said he would help remove the filters that color my perspective. I see a vision of myself sitting in a small enclosing. The filters are prongs like those on a fork. They hang like bars in front of me, pinning me in.

Just yesterday the Lord lifted one prong to help me reveal my true inner self—as I gave him permission to do after a conversation I had with a friend. She'd commented that I once resented having to work so hard to bring in the finances to support David and me.

"What?" I questioned.

"You said that the other day," she reminded me. *Oh,* I thought. *Did I say that out loud?* Why yes, I believe I did. But to hear it said back to me was jarring.

As I continue to sit in the sauna, I follow the trail of that conversation, acknowledging that, for most of our married life, I resented how David didn't work in a secular job. He was a minister, but the ministry work did not bring in the funds to support us. My work in adult literacy paid most of our bills. Plus, after putting in hours at that job, I then ministered alongside David. I had no break, and I felt I was working harder than him. The arrangement was supposed to be temporary, just until income from the ministry built up enough for me to leave my job. That never happened. And even though David and I agreed on this arrangement, it bothered me. If anyone ever questioned it or commented on it, I became defensive. Obviously, my inner self did not match what I was portraying on the outside. I acted like I was good with the arrangement. I wasn't.

I bring my attention back to the Lord and our current conversation in the sauna. I'm uncomfortable with this truth. But in the end, I feel it is good. It does not take anything away from David and me; it is just the way things were—the good, the bad, and the . . . other.

"I get it," I say to the Lord.

"Yes, you do. Now breathe deeply. Lift your arms and inhale.

"See how your rib cage lifts and your body opens to take in more air? It's good to lift your arms—for praise, for trust, and for your health. It's good."

"Yes, it's good," I agree as I continue to raise my arms in praise and thanksgiving and appreciation for deep breathing. "It is good," I whisper, taking in and savoring yet another breath and then sending the stale air of what I once hid in my heart out and away.

Chapter 10

Hope Pulled Off a Shelf

"It's been a rough morning," I say to the Lord. Today I'm not going to get on the treadmill. I'm not going into the sauna. I don't want to. I sit in the chair beside my bedroom window, looking out at the gray sky. "I can't seem to find my place," I continue.

"God, I'm mad at you. I'm mad. No reason. I just am." I sit quietly, wondering where this is coming from.

"I know," God answers. "I knew before you did, and I understand."

I keep looking at my hands—the hands of an old woman. Wrinkled, flabby, full of age spots. They're old and tired, and I hate to look at them. I lotion them, slowly running my fingers along the veins and stretching out the skin to make it smooth. Then it pops back into wrinkle city as soon as I lift my finger. My hands show years of use and abuse. I'm mad.

"Lord, I read in a devotional this morning that I should praise you and give thanks. But the praise and the thanks are stuck in my throat. They come out in low guttural moans of angst, complaint, and wordless pain. There's my praise. That's the most I can seem to muster today."

"Truth sounds like that," he says. "There was a time when

you would stop what you were feeling and saying and put on the facade you thought I expected from you. And you would begin to just say, 'Praise you, thank you, blah, blah, blah.' That would lift your spirits, and then you would go on about your activity, casting aside the real stirring that was in your heart.

"That's not really praise, not of a true heart. I'd rather hear the groaning."

"And then what?" I ask. "So I groan and feel sad and angry. Then what?"

These days I'm a little stumped, a little confused. I used to think I had the answers. I thought I was doing well to ignore or suppress feelings. I believed we weren't supposed to be led by our feelings, only by our spirits, as if feelings were bad and needed to be overcome. I thought that if I would just confess these thoughts and feelings as sin, saying they were not me, I'd be free of them.

But now? I think I was wrong. I think feelings do have purpose and need to be taken into account somehow. I don't think it's healthy, or spiritual, to regard feelings as something evil, something about which to repent. Is it?

"Look deeper," the Lord says. "Look into the feeling, like looking into your reflection in a lake. What do you see?"

"I see I'm tired, and I feel lost. I see these abused old hands fit me—spotted and wrinkled, with the elasticity of hope sucked out. Where did it go?"

"It went south, as they say. It all went south. The hope you bought was pulled off a shelf, prepackaged. It was the descriptions, the dreams, the mantras, the beliefs about what is good and desirable and what to look forward to in the future. Is that your hope? Nah. That hope was what others told you to take in as hope. You're already seeing now that a prepackaged version will not satisfy you.

"True hope—hope that is yours—is born out of pain, out of grief, out of letting life touch you and cut into the most tender flesh of your heart. Hope knows that you do not have to pretend those pains and disappointments don't exist, or that they don't matter. It is owning them, feeling them, naming them. If you do not first own them and name them, then you cannot leave and move away from them. You will carry them with you, and they will snuff out hope.

"You're angry because you bought a package of hope because it was cheap. It didn't require much from you to pull it from the shelf. You said, 'This will do. This is me.' As is so often said in the world, you get what you pay for. That package was a knockoff, not the real thing.

"Stop. Let the groans come and tell you from whence they come. Let them tell you what it is within you that daily cuts away a sliver of hope and disfigures your dreams. Speak it. Name it."

I sit in silence and let the weight of this conversation rest on me. Then I glance out the window as the maple tree catches my attention. Its leaves begin to sway ever so lightly. I want to be like a leaf on that tree, snug and secure and without fear. Without toiling and struggling to stay connected to the branch. Confident that it is right where it belongs.

Me? I feel lost. I'm not confident about where I am. I don't know who I am because that person was never allowed to take form. Rather, I constantly morphed into what I thought was expected of me. And now, without expectations drawing me, I don't know how to perform. I don't know what I'm to do. I don't know how I'm supposed to act. But I know that I'm angry.

"Lord," I say as my breath settles into the bottom of my heart and I search for words, "I think those groanings say that what I thought was me is no more. What is me can now come forth. It's time to show up and see who I am.

"So, Lord, thank you for this moment, this conversation, this enlightenment, and this hope. I do give you thanks."

He gives me a wink, and I wink back. We smile.

Chapter 11

The Secret Garden

Coffee. It's midmorning, and I'm longing for a fresh cup. I reach into the back of the cupboard and pull out my handy little grinder to grind some fresh coffee beans. As I set it on the kitchen counter, I notice a large dispenser of some sort of solution sitting next to a box of baking soda. My roommate Kathleen must have been in earlier. She likely prepared some holistic remedy for some reason.

Then whoosh! I start crying.

Out of the blue, I flash back to five years earlier when I turned my kitchen counter into a laboratory of sorts. My husband had peritonitis, a serious infection connected with his peritoneal dialysis treatment. The dialysis clinic staff had shown me how to mix the powder antibiotic with a liquid and inject it into his dialysis solution bags. The steps to follow were all so very specific, and I had to be oh so careful not to contaminate the needle or the bag or anything.

Me. Me, who is not a medically savvy person. Me, who is not comfortable with such work. Me, alone in my kitchen.

As the memory comes to me now, I cry, and with the tears comes a release of all the tension that accompanied that task

—tension I never voiced or was even aware of until this moment. That responsibility to care for my husband in a life-or-death situation terrified me, but I had to do it. I felt so alone, but I had to do it. And I did it.

Now, as tears fall five years later, that tension has unveiled itself.

I recall the conversation I had with God earlier this morning. He said, "You know, there is no good thing that I would keep from you. As this awareness seeps deeply into your heart, you will begin to reciprocate; and I will know there is no good thing you would keep from me." I was in awe as I pondered that statement.

"Everything about you is good," he continued. "I desire all from you, to know you with no secrets between us. I desire to sit with you, face-to-face, and to look at your smile as you take my hand and say yes."

No secrets between us.

"Yes," the Lord says, bringing me back to this moment. "With your tears you've uncovered that which has been kept secret from even you, and that secret built a small wall between us. Not tall enough that I could not see you or you see me, but a small rising out of the ground that was enough to stub your toe and trip you as you came nearer to me."

"I was afraid," I say. "I was so afraid."

In speaking these words, I understand a tension that lifts with them. This emotion of being afraid and feeling left alone to handle David's care hardened a part of me—not only emotionally but also physically. It hardened the physical cells of my being. This morning I'm softening. I feel the tenderness of God's love as my cells begin to rebalance and heal. Life's flow begins to seep more freely through those living vessels.

"That is one secret we won't stumble on anymore," the Lord says. "That is one secret that held you at a distance from me. I waited patiently for you, and now you've responded.

That has opened a doorway to more that you have desired. Consider it a door to a secret garden."

"Ah." I smile. *The Secret Garden* was my favorite childhood book. It mesmerized me, and I always wanted a secret garden, a hidden place where I could explore and find treasures of life and beauty. A place hidden away from shame and fear.

"The secret of your garden is that it is not hidden away. It's not secret. Your garden is in plain sight where all can see and all can know. It is where your secrets no longer bind your soul. In this garden you lay bare before the world. It is where you freely walk about and enjoy the garden's wonder without care, concern, or awareness of what anyone else is seeing or saying. There your attention can turn outward to life itself and not be held captive to the task of preserving secrets.

"This is what you have desired," the Lord says. "This is what has opened within you. As we continue to unlock what is hidden, your body will cease to carry such burdens that weigh you down and damage your cells. Rather, life will flow. Love will flow, and your garden will flourish. I look forward to walking in that garden with you."

I wipe away the final tear and smile. I look forward to that also.

Chapter 12

For Singing Out Loud

"Good morning, Lord. Hey, I just heard myself singing . . . out loud," I say in surprise as I walk into the kitchen and consider what to prepare for dinner. That has not happened in a very long time. I'm amused. Curious.

"Yes," he responds. "I am also amused. But not curious. I know where the singing is coming from. Your heart and your soul are becoming untangled. Those fears and unspoken secrets—unknown even to you—are being loosed. They can no longer choke and stifle your joy."

"I'm glad to hear this, Lord."

I suddenly become oh so tired. My eyes want to close, and I want to drift to sleep. Maybe that's to let the healing continue, to let it take place. Keeping secrets, even unintentionally hidden ones, requires so much attention. It is very draining on the soul. Somehow, I know instinctively that this untangling process requires a lot of energy; not conscious energy, but energy at the cellular level while my body adapts to truth, to reality. It requires energy at the mental level while I wrap my mind around new ideas.

Everything inside moves to support what is true and let

go of—detox and cleanse—what is not true, what is not me. The cells realign to drive out what has been hanging on inside —the lies stuck to the walls, hiding, controlling, redirecting, and stifling life. It's a very active process.

I take a calm breath and smile as I consider this wonderful marvel of being human. My head swirls with what I've been hearing and learning in these recent conversations. I don't have to try to be perfect, to live up to anyone's expectations, including my own. I don't have to pretend I'm fearless and have it all together when I'm really feeling afraid. I can relax.

"Now life can flow," the Lord says.

"I know. I can feel it." I close my eyes and sit for a moment at the kitchen table while I think about this new journey I'm on. I'm grateful for these intimate discussions with my Lord. It is all so simple, so easy now.

I open the refrigerator and pull out ingredients for tonight's dinner. Lettuce, tomatoes, cilantro, and onion. As I chop them, I think about music. I've played music most of my life—piano, flute, and guitar. I even have a bachelor's degree in music. I've never played at a professional level but well enough to occasionally entertain friends and lead worship in ministry gatherings. Mostly though, I've used music to console myself in troublesome times. I lost that joy somewhere. I don't play anymore. I don't sing. That's why it's so interesting to me that I'm singing this morning. I hope it will continue. It's nice.

"That joy is still there," the Lord whispers, "and it will surface more as you continue to open your heart. It's a process, and you're doing well."

"Thank you, Lord."

I hum as I turn my attention to cooking a pound of ground beef for the tacos I'm making. It's dinnertime, and I'm hungry.

Chapter 13

Alive and Blessed to Be Alive

I thank God I'm alive. I'm truly blessed.

"That hasn't always been the case," the Lord says, dropping by as I sit in my chair at the window, preparing to start my day. "You've always been alive, but not always thankful."

"Guilty," I say.

I have given so much time and attention to all that's wrong. Never satisfied. Living by the spirit of *Oh well.* Afraid to believe. Afraid to desire. Afraid to hope because, surely, my hopes couldn't be. They would never happen, so these hopes were passed off as unimportant. Downplayed.

I didn't get picked for the team. Oh well, it's not like I have time for it anyway.

I gained five pounds instead of losing five. Oh well, it's not a good time to try. Maybe after the holidays.

The money didn't come through for my trip. Oh well, it wasn't that important. Maybe I'll go next year.

I've accepted these stories I made up. They alleviate the pain of unmet expectations. Well, at least some of the pain; that which is on the surface. But if I look closely, or sit still long enough, the truth emerges: I am disappointed. Further, my faith is shaken, and it's hard to believe. I limit expectations. I curate desires, choosing to only allow those that I think might really have a chance. I set fewer goals because, after all, it's easier to not want than to not get.

Now I'm awake. I'm willing to believe, to want, and to be honest about those desires. It scares me, sure. But that's part of being alive, isn't it? That's part of being aware. It's a risk to go after a dream, to not give up when it doesn't quickly appear, but I'm gaining courage. I think my dreams are worth going after. That's part of the beauty of this life. It makes living it all the more precious.

"Yes, and that's the beauty of uncovering secrets that trip you up," the Lord interjects into my reflections. "Once you're aware of them, you can do something about them. You can step beyond them. You no longer need to hide."

Chapter 14

No Baby

This afternoon I step into the dry sauna to release some toxins and have some quiet time with my Lord. He brings me back to a conversation we've had about secrets. So, while physically I sit in the sauna, spiritually I move to the picnic table in the meadow, to my favorite spot. The Lord and I do some digging through my secrets.

"What's in your heart?" the Lord asks me.

"A dead baby." I'm surprised by my answer. That thought was not in my conscious mind. "No, I don't mean a *dead* baby, but just the fact of never having had a child." I flounder, trying to find the words. It's not that I ever particularly desired to have children; I've never been the motherly type. So not having children was not such a big deal to me.

In more recent years it has comforted me that many couples these days don't have children. The pressure is released just a little in knowing that I'm not the only one. It seems society expects that once you marry, you'll have children. It's the normal flow of life. Maybe it's not even society; maybe it was just my expectation. Regardless, I felt out of step with the world.

"Tell me more about it," the Lord encourages. "Why did you not desire children?"

I take a deep breath. This discussion hasn't come out of the blue. Last week I was at a concert by the Isaacs. I love their music. One of the sisters shared about losing a baby and thinking she would never have a child; I could feel her overwhelming sadness, and I could feel her joy that she ended up giving birth to two children.

Then on a television program last night, I heard two women share about how they chose, deliberately, not to have children. They each felt they could not fulfill what they wanted to do and also be good mothers. So they made conscious decisions not to have children. I never did that. I just drifted into not having children.

My mind starts rolling. Is it true that I really did not care about having children? That was never my stated decision.

"So why, then?"

"It just wasn't a passion for me."

"And what is the reason for that?" He keeps digging.

"I was afraid I couldn't," I respond. "I didn't want to be disappointed or for David to be disappointed if we decided to have children and then couldn't."

David and I both had physical conditions that made it impossible—or at least unlikely—for us to have children. We hoped for a miracle. Then through the years, as we remained childless, we changed our story. "We're okay without children. It's not that big of a deal for us." Lately, the topic seems to be circling me. And now even the Lord has brought it up!

I become nauseous. I feel weak with sorrow. I turn off the sauna but stay seated, with the door open and cool air blowing in as I continue the conversation.

"Fear. I was afraid," I say.

"And why were you afraid?" the Lord presses.

"Unworthiness," I hear myself reply. "I never felt worthy to be a mother, to be trusted with a life."

The secret lie begins to unravel. I was afraid I wasn't good enough, that I would not be a good mother. Maybe God wouldn't give me a child. Over time, I created the cover story that I wasn't really interested in having children. It was a good story. Heck, I believed it!

There was a time in my mid-thirties when I thought I might be pregnant. Just maybe. I went to the doctor to find out, and the test was negative. I was not pregnant. *Oh, okay,* I thought. *That's all right, I just needed to know.*

I bought it, that it was okay, until I began walking across the parking lot to my car. I almost fell to the ground. My knees started to buckle under me. That's when I realized that I did want to be pregnant, that I was hoping for the test to be positive. I sat in my car, alone, and cried.

In our early years people would lay hands on me and David and pray for us to conceive. Over time, I began to feel shame because I couldn't get pregnant. I felt like I was letting everyone down. Finally, there came a point when prayers no longer encouraged me; they only made me mad, made me feel inadequate. They only shined a spotlight on my barrenness. The issue was easier to deal with once I was past childbearing years. Thankfully, people stopped laying hands on me and praying for a pregnancy.

Now I'm uncovering the truth. It was a big deal. Now I see that it is something I couldn't look at. Instead, I dressed up this weed as some new exotic flower. I cultivated it and grew it in my own personal garden. I let others see it and believe that it was a precious flower.

Standing now in full sun, I can see that the lie that I did not want children is only an unwanted weed. I wish I had not hidden the desire to be a mother. I would have liked to have had children.

"I suppose we need to pull this weed, this lie I've told," I say to the Lord. "How do we do that?"

"You don't need to pull it," the Lord says. "Just let it sit there and it will wither away and disappear. Now that you have named it for what it is and stopped calling it some special kind of flower. Now that it is seen in truth and light, it has lost its power, its life force. You're free from it. Its pain will wither and blow away."

Part Three

Growing Roots

Chapter 15

Everybody Loves Cathay

"**A**lways assume that people love you," the Lord says as I walk across the horse pasture deep in thought, stepping carefully so I don't fall prey to the uneven ground trying to catch me off balance. "Always start from there," he says.

I welcome the conversation. Today I'm once again feeling a little displaced, like I don't know where I belong. I feel lost.

It occurs to me that I have always approached new situations and new people timidly, anticipating that they may not like me or we may not connect. That I may not fit in. I hold back in a wait-and-see posture, which pretty much guarantees I won't fit in. Interesting, huh? *Wait-and-see* leaves you hanging on the sidelines or trailing behind. So I perk up when the Lord says this to me.

"Assume everyone loves me? That feels rather arrogant, Lord."

"Not really. I love you, and if I love you, how can anyone else not? Park the arrogance there," he says. "Let me be the arrogant one. I am confident enough and know you well enough to say that this is the belief from which you should approach life. Everybody loves Cathay."

That's a simple thought, and I can't find a reason to debate it. What if it really is that simple? And really, why should I start any new situation or relationship believing otherwise? Still, the very notion of that approach leaves me twisting inside, as if a rodeo cowboy has lassoed my intestines with a lariat and is gently tugging at them—tugging me out of my comfort zone. Assuming that everybody loves me has never been my base self-concept.

"You have to take it on faith," the Lord says, interrupting my internal monologue. "Just assume it because I told you to. It's not about whether it's true. It's only about what you believe. I'm telling you to believe this."

I slowly commit that I am willing to do that. As I meet people, I will assume they all just absolutely love me. Oh God. That scares the hell out of me. Makes me feel a bit queasy. Seriously? Oh my.

I ponder the idea as I walk back across the pasture and toward the house. If I approach people thinking that they may not like me, then my energies go into protecting myself or trying to be likable. That attitude can send out negative vibes and make people feel put off.

On the other hand, if I assume people like me, then I can focus my energy on them. The fact that they like and accept me is already established—at least in my mind. That's not so arrogant. It's just a rearrangement of perspective and focus.

"Did you get that little twist there?" I say to the Lord, ready to bring him back into the conversation.

"Yes. Nice twist," he answers.

I think into it further and apply the logic to God too. It occurs to me that if I come to God believing he absolutely loves and adores me, then I can be free and honest and respond with total love and openness. If I approach in guilt, shame, and fear that God is not happy with me, I won't be able to receive or return the love. My energies will be tied up in hiding, in creating stories and excuses, all because I assumed he was disappointed in me. Hmm. Now that's an arrogant assumption.

I think I get it. If I'm going to make assumptions, I'm better off assuming that God—and everybody—loves me. I commit to try that on.

Chapter 16

The Reluctant Pioneer

I know there is yet a lot for me to live here on the earth. I have a purpose and a mission. I have life. Yet sometimes that zest for life, that pull of my purpose, the direction for the journey, eludes me. As I sit at my bedroom window pondering this thought, I have a vision in which I sit on a rock—a large stone fashioned as a chair just for me, at the edge of a road. As I take a seat, I think about where I am.

"You're here with me," the Lord says, answering the question I didn't voice. "You're here. Alive and growing more and more alive each day. The power is within you to grasp hold of realities that you cannot see with your eyes. It is within your reach, but you shrink from it. You wait."

I'm reminded of my career. In my adult literacy work I always rose to positions of director or manager but never to the top. That was a conscious decision. I didn't want to be the one leading the way. I liked being second in charge. I wanted at least one person in a position above me to take the heat, to be responsible, as it were. I could support that person and move the organization forward, but its ultimate result did not depend on me. I liked being a follower. I liked being part of a cozy group, invisibly nestled among peers, waiting for direction. Evidently, that's what I still like.

"Is that where I am now?" I ask my Lord. "Waiting for someone else to come forward? Someone I can follow down the road?"

"Yeah, something like that," he says. "You're not too keen on blazing your own trail."

"That's true," I say.

"First, you need to understand that blazing a trail does not mean everything depends on you. It's not a burden. It can be an exciting and joyful process. Walk your road wherever it takes you. There's no set path you must find. At the same time, others will walk their paths. They're not following you. As each one moves in faith individually, all are lifted together. Some paths run parallel, some cross, some repeat the same ground one behind another. All rise to their journey, our journey. It really is all one journey, one life, one faith.

"Don't worry about blazing a trail. Don't fear being a pioneer. Just set out to walk your path. Sometimes that will be a new trail, and you will require ingenuity to proceed. Other times you will travel over roads that others have already carved. You're equipped for both."

Today is not the first time I've received this gentle coaching about being a pioneer. In the early 1980s, I sang as a guest on a local radio show. A few months later, I had a radio show of my own, *The Word in Song*. What is most remarkable is how this unfolded.

I was getting dressed to go to a friend's house for a jubilee, an evening of music making. As I picked up my guitar to leave, I heard the Lord say to me, "Someone is going to invite you to come and sing tomorrow. I want you to say yes." It being Saturday, I assumed someone would invite me to sing at a church service the next morning. Further, I knew the Lord was wise to prepare me ahead of time, telling me to accept the invitation. Otherwise, shyness would have likely taken over, causing me to say no. At the party, someone did invite me to sing the next day—not at his church but on his Sunday morning radio program.

Good thing I had been prepared or I definitely would have declined.

Guitar in hand, I calmed my nerves and sang two songs on that show. It energized me. I felt at home, and I wanted more of that experience. The host invited me back two more times. Then a month later he canceled his program. I asked the station for his ten o'clock Sunday morning time slot so I could host a show of my own, and they granted it. The ministry I worked with sponsored the show: fifteen minutes of singing and sharing testimonies, prerecorded each week.

Days before the first recordings I felt anxious and nervous. I was overwhelmed. Clearly, I was in over my head. *What was I ever thinking?*

Talking about it with one of the ministry elders, he spoke a prophetic word to me. In that word he called me the *reluctant pioneer*. That stuck with me. It makes me laugh to realize it's still an appropriate moniker. *The reluctant pioneer.* Just as meaningful today as it was forty years ago.

"Yes, the *reluctant pioneer*," the Lord says to me. "But even though you've been reluctant, at least you have continued to move forward. This is good. I'm pleased with you."

"So I should get up off this rock and keep moving, I suppose."

"Yes. And honestly, the direction of your path does not elude you. You know where you're going. You're just acting like your usual reluctant self, and you're dragging your feet for effect."

We laugh. That pretty much nails it.

The laughter lightens the weight of the vision. I smile. It's okay. I know that I can press on. It occurs to me I might even give up my reluctance. Just maybe.

Chapter 17

The Mountain Before Me

Today I've gotten back into my routine: a workout followed by a twenty-minute sauna session. As I sit on the wooden bench and let myself relax in the heat, I close my eyes and step into a vision. I walk to my favorite picnic table in the meadow where my Lord is sitting. He's waiting for me. As I draw near my eyes move to the mountain in the distance. A very tall mountain reaching into the clouds. The Lord is looking at it too. It is a beautiful vision, but I catch a glimpse of another scene there. I see myself scaling up the rigid sides of this towering mountain. I don't like what I see. I feel apprehensive.

"Oh no, I should have guessed," I say with a heavy sigh. "This can't be good." I'm in awe of how people scale the sides of mountains, holding on to who knows what and slipping their fingers into little crevices that can barely be seen. It is a daunting challenge to me. Something I could never do, and something I have no interest in now.

"No," the Lord responds. He reaches across the table and takes my hands in his. "I would never ask you to go climb that mountain alone. Never." He lets me know that our relationship is not born out of a Hollywood script. It's not what I've seen in movies. He will not task me to perform some impossible feat. To be like a superhero called into service to save the world. Alone. All by myself.

"I would never send you alone on a mission—a dangerous, nearly impossible quest. I won't test you. I won't ask anything of you just to please me. I will never ask that.

"When it's time to climb the mountain—and there will come a time," he adds, "I will go with you. We will ascend it together, hand in hand."

"Part of that pioneer training? A little trail blazing?" I ask with a smile, anxious to show I've been listening. I'm getting used to the idea. Starting to think it may even be fun. Well, tomorrow it might be fun. I'm still not ready today. Thankfully, I can see that my Lord knows this.

"You are a pioneer. Don't let the title scare you," he says.

I know, but I'm still reluctant.

Chapter 18

The Refreshing

No picnic table today. As I physically enter my sauna time, my spirit slips into a natural hot spring with my Lord. Nestled in among the stones cuddling the warm waters, we sit looking at each other, gazing without words just like David and I used to do. After years of marriage, we often needed no words between us. Sometimes he would slightly nod his head, as if to reaffirm, *It's okay.* Sometimes I would be tempted to ask him what he was thinking, but then I'd realize there was no need. It was soothing to just sit together without chatter. That's the way I feel today sitting in the hot spring with my Lord.

I lean my head back against the edge of the stone bank and let the waters slowly glide across my shoulders. Healing waters. Calming waters.

Then the Lord says a strange thing to me. He wants me to schedule a foot massage. "I want you to tend to your feet," he says. "Your feet are tired. You've walked a long way, and you have a great journey yet ahead of you. You need feet that are cared for, strong feet, feet that will take you far."

"Is that because I have to climb that mountain?" I tease.

"Would that make a difference?" he counters. "Do you

need a reason? If it is because of the mountain ahead, does that mean you won't care for your feet? In protest? In fear?"

"The thought crossed my mind," I say sheepishly.

"So many questions. So many worries. Stop and return your attention to the warmth and comfort of the hot spring. Let the waters wash over you. And if you don't want a foot massage, you don't have to get one."

"No, I'm down for the massage, Lord. I guess I was just trying to stir up trouble. Sometimes it's hard to relax, and my mind goes off on these tangents. Remember, I'm the *reluctant pioneer.*"

He smiles. "I know. Close your eyes and let the waters sweep over you. Maybe they'll cleanse some of that reluctance away. Besides, as I already said, I'm with you, and you have nothing to fear."

That's reassuring. I appreciate the Lord's tender touch and the way he is always looking out for my good, always preparing me for what's ahead. Ever faithful.

Chapter 19

—————

Learning to Believe

No pre-sauna workout today. Nope. I took two steps on the treadmill, and it stopped. It broke. The belt would no longer turn.

So, I move on to the sauna and I sit. *Why did that break?* I wonder. I feel bad because not only did the treadmill break, but yesterday the citrus juicer burned out while I was using it. I think I've always been a bit leery of mechanical things, afraid I'll break them.

"There you have it," the Lord says. "Do you remember when you would confidently walk up and speak to broken things? Then you expected them to work again. And sometimes they did!"

"Yes."

"I remember that too. I remember that person. Where did you go?"

"Good question," I say. "I got smart. So smart that I thought I knew everything. That I should just take care of business and not bother you with it. But that's not working so well. I think there is something off in my doctrine."

"You think?" he says, not really asking. Just stating the obvious.

In my earlier years I often laid hands on others and saw them recover. I once prayed about a car not functioning and suddenly knew what was wrong with it. I've known faith. Then, I suppose I fell into a common trap—I came up with a formula for it. No longer free flowing, prayer included a list of rules and procedures to follow.

Over time I was seeing fewer and fewer results. Nothing would happen. I began to doubt myself. I became unsure of my beliefs. I forgot how to just pray and believe.

The good news is my faith is being restored. God and I are together, me in him and him in me. I still have a lot to learn, but I am encouraged.

Chapter 20

Rolling with God

We're rolling now—new treadmill, new hope, and a new appreciation for God and his wondrous love! Today I finish my workout and go to the sauna to talk with my Lord, eager to hear what he might say to me and me to him.

Sure enough, when I get to the sauna and settle in, I see the Lord. He's sitting in our special spot. The picnic table at the edge of the meadow is so welcoming. As I walk toward him, I try to find the words to articulate what's on my mind. Prayer and faith, the kind that produces results. I've been thinking more about it. Just what is it, really? How does it work?

For many years I've followed a belief that God is on sabbath. He is resting and not active. That he created the earth, fully equipped us with all we need to subdue it and live in it abundantly, and then took his leave. He gave us all the tools we need to prosper. He expects us to use them and not be running to him for help.

In the past year on a few occasions, I called out for God's help because I didn't know what else to do. I stopped acting like I knew everything and acknowledged that I didn't know anything. Feeling nothing within me to draw from, I asked God for help and guidance—and those prayers were answered. They did produce results.

Now I'm gaining some clarity. I'm growing some roots. I am relieved to know that God did not leave; he is still right here with me, through all of this journey and awakening. Us together, in vibrational oneness, produces results and answers prayer. I'm not alone and never will be. We're a team.

That's my frame of mind as I somberly walk to the picnic bench to sit with the Lord. "I've been trying to live independently, and to pray for people and for myself, with faith in what you have already given, not asking for your help," I say to open the conversation with the Lord. "But it's not been working very well."

I got to the place where I hardly prayed at all. I could no longer get it to work. My faith was ineffectual, ungrounded. Now I've found I can have a free-flowing relationship with God, and I'm enjoying the experience. I know it's time to take my alone time with him and carry it into all areas of my daily life.

"It's okay," he says, knowing my every thought. "It's good to see you. It's been a while."

"I know," I respond softly. "I was a bit overwhelmed with all we've been discussing. I think I needed time to let it digest. Or maybe I was preferring to avoid it. I'm not sure which."

"You've been on quite a learning journey," he says, taking my hand in his.

We sit in silence. The sun's warmth feels good on my skin, good on my heart.

"I'll go with you," he says. "Always. You don't have to do it alone. Don't go out there without me."

I nod in agreement and rest my head on his shoulder.

Chapter 21

The Line of Scrimmage

Finishing my shower this morning, I ask, "What do I need to know about today, Lord?"

"You've reached the line of scrimmage," he answers. *The line of scrimmage?* I played flute in my high school band *back in the day*, which means I went to football games and am somewhat familiar with the sport. I still like to watch it from time to time. No favorite teams, but I can appreciate a good game. I think for a moment about what it means to be at the line of scrimmage. I recall that it's an invisible line across the football field where the ball is placed to start a play. What strikes me as important is that a team cannot cross that line until the ball is snapped and the next play begins.

"Perfect!" I say. "Coach, you're letting me know that you're working on something, and I should just chill until you get the next play set up, eh?" (I've been using *eh?* a lot lately. This Canadian expression looks and sounds so much better than the American *huh?* To my ears *eh* sounds light and uplifting, whereas *huh* sounds dull and lifeless.)

"Yes," he says. "I could have simply said that you've done all I've given you to do and should now just stand. Be still and wait. But I thought you'd enjoy the football reference more."

"And I do!"

"With the line of scrimmage reference," he continues, "you can visually see that the game is still on. There is still activity. There is still more to come. We're in just a brief pause while teams refocus and set up the next play.

"I know that gives you hope and clarity. If I were to tell you to be still and wait, I know you would. But I also know you would become impatient. Your mind would wander. You would question and doubt and maybe even get worked up . . . "

"Over nothing," I say, finishing his sentence. "Lord, I get it. I get what you're telling me. I'll chill—though I suspect that is really not a good phrase either, eh? Let me say it simply, I'll be still and wait."

I like this visual. I think it will be quite helpful in future days to equate *being still and waiting* with not crossing the line of scrimmage until the next play is in action. I do seem to be at a new time in my life. I sense my purpose. My focus is becoming clearer, and that has made me anxious. I want to rush ahead and get on with it. I want to have everything clearly laid out.

Ha! And not so long ago I was writing about how I appreciate and can enjoy ambiguity! I only fooled myself. I only appreciated living in ambiguity for a brief moment. I laugh.

The Lord laughs with me. "A very brief moment, eh?"

"Lord, you've certainly got your hands full. I do trust you and know that you are putting together the next play. You're the coach, and you see the game from a fuller viewpoint. You know what needs to be in place before you release me to cross the line and do my part. I'll wait . . . patiently."

What's my part? I wonder as I continue musing over the metaphor. I used to play football. In my much younger days I enjoyed playing. It was usually flag football, sometimes tackle —just in the neighborhood with friends or maybe at school during PE class. I recall taking the position of guard. Not the center, not the quarterback, not the wing running down the field to score the winning touchdown, but guard. I would do what was necessary (hopefully) to protect the quarterback while he or she did their thing to get that ball moving. Is that my role? In matters of the spirit?

Part Four

Blooming

Chapter 22

Push Harder

"Push," the Lord says. "Push harder. Walk farther. Speak louder. Think deeper. In other words, don't stop now."

"What? What's that about?" I'm not really asking for clarification. I'm simply filling the silence in my mind as I set up my towel to sit for a bit in the sauna. The Lord has gotten a jump on me this morning. No easing into the day's chat. Looks like we're getting right to the gist of it.

"I'm getting you primed, ready for action before you start dragging your feet, dragging them loud enough, hard enough, to distract you from hearing my voice. You tend to do that when you think you know what may be ahead and you don't want to face it."

"I guess that's clear enough, eh Lord? You know me pretty well." I'm amused with myself at the way I do that. Resistance is my default response to everything. I rarely hear a suggestion and jump up all excited about it. I'm slow to get on board and embrace new ideas.

On the other hand, I do like an adventure once I get moving. I do like to set off in some direction not knowing where I'll end up. I do like walking into the unknown. Even though the outward persona I've developed is seemingly quiet and unsure and wanting stability and little change, I know that's not my true heart. That's not really me, but that's the one who drags her feet at the suggestion of anything new.

"Yes," the Lord interjects. "It's time to stop and recalibrate. Set your feet under you, and let's go."

"I appreciate this shove-off for today, Lord. I can hardly wait to see what's coming."

"And I appreciate that you're willing to listen, willing to move," he tells me. "Far too many people get stopped alongside the road, tired and empty. They just lay down, content to remain there, never coming into the purpose of the journey. Never coming to know where that road will lead them. You might say the road is littered with half-lived lives.

"Too many give up their dreams, their callings, way too early. Some stop before they even start. Others get sidetracked and then back away, unsure and not quite remembering where they were going. And others simply determine it is not worth the effort to keep walking. Sadly, they don't even lift their eyes up off the road to see the end of the trail. They decide it is worthless without even looking at what it is! They sell short their inheritance, their place in the world, their joy, their sense of well-being, of relationship, of life. I call and I call. They sit and they sit. Motionless. Fearful and quiet, lest anyone should ask anything of them."

"I've seen that," I say, then sadly add, "I've done that. Too often I've stopped short of the goal because I'm afraid of what lays down the road, just around the curve or over the hill."

"I know," he says, "and you're tempted to pull back now. That's why I'm telling you to push harder. You're at the edge of breaking through to living fully. This is no time to stop and rest. Not today."

"That's something worth pushing for," I say quietly. I know it's so. I can feel it just as assuredly as I feel the sweet sauna heat engulfing my body and sweat beading across my brow.

I close my eyes and let the message sink in. I sit still. It's time to recalibrate, to stop dragging my feet. It's time to fully embrace life.

Chapter 23

Riding in the Canoe

I feel like something is changing in me and something will be changing up ahead. I close my eyes as I sit in my window chair and turn to the Lord. In a vision I see myself walking by a small, gently flowing river when the Lord comes alongside me. He's traveling in a canoe. "Get inside," he says, paddling to the bank where I stand. "Ride with me for a while."

I'm nervous about this narrow canoe. I think about its potential to capsize. "No," I say. "I'll just keep walking here to the side."

I'm on a narrow but clearly marked dirt path. Stones and grass sometimes cover it over, but it's still easy to walk. I'm comfortable on it, comfortable moving forward on the power of my own two feet. I'm not comfortable trusting anyone or anything else. I like to be in control of where I set my feet. It's all on me. Whether good or bad, it's all on me.

Then the Lord points out what I don't want to hear. "That's working fine for now, but up ahead your trail is cut off. There's no way to continue on ground alongside the river. You'll have to cut off and go up the mountain. That's a long and a hard way to go. Come on," he invites again, "Get in the canoe, and I'll take you around that patch. Then you can disembark on the other side where the river joins soft land again."

Not what I want to hear. Evidently, I can't continue on this path as I am. Something has to change. Though it gives me pause, I acknowledge that the canoe is the better way to go.

"Okay, Lord. I'm in," I respond, somewhat reluctantly.

I step into the canoe while he steadies it. As we set off, I'm filled with relief. It really is okay. Okay to change the path. Okay to do something different. Okay to trust someone else. Okay to rest from my efforts.

It really is okay.

Chapter 24

Climbing the Mountain

Sitting in the warm, toasty sauna, I have a vision in which I start to climb a mountain—the mountain I've seen in previous visions. The one I've known I would eventually need to face. At the beginning there's a nice little trail on a ledge circling its spire. It's just wide enough to comfortably hike. But no, it's not for me. The Lord comes up and says, "Let's go up this way." He guides my hands to small crevices and rocks jetting from the mountain face. We begin to scale up the side.

"Oh no, Lord. Really?"

"Really," he responds. "You can do it. I'm here with you in it."

"Why not just walk on the well-formed trail?"

"That's not your path; this one holds greater joy for you."

"Yeah, right," I mutter.

So up the side of the mountain we go. Me doing things I never dreamed possible. Slowly. Carefully. Before long, we get to a small, flat ledge, and the Lord helps me up to sit on it. We rest. The sky is so blue, so vividly blue. White, big-bellied clouds float nearby. I turn my gaze downward and see the well-honed trail below. People are easily passing by on it.

"Wouldn't it be better to just walk that road, Lord?" I try again. "We'd certainly move a little faster."

"Faster? Getting to the end? Is that your focus? There's more to life. Getting to the end quickly does not serve your purpose. It's not your reason for life. Sit and rest with me."

We sit. We rest. Then my mind does what it so often does when I'm sitting and resting, trying to enter stillness. It imagines.

I imagine I get so rested that my body releases all tension and loses all form. It starts to slide. Left unchecked I would simply drift off the ledge, down onto the welcoming trail below.

From the corner of my eye, I catch the Lord's glance. No words, no shaking of the head, but his glance says it all.

His eyes say, *Really?* It's an endearing look, one eyebrow raised, with love and appreciation for me and for my awkwardness. He doesn't need to say anything. I sit up, pull my shoulders back, and wait.

"If you were on the path below, you would miss so much," the Lord says. "It's not about getting somewhere. I want you to see and appreciate life here. Be alive in the moment in which you are living."

"I get it," I say. Well, I don't really get it because if I did, he wouldn't have to keep telling me things like this. But for right now, this moment, I get it.

Then I take in a deep breath, and the awareness of the 126-degree heat surrounding me in the sauna pulls me into the present. It feels wonderful. I sit and soak it in with appreciation and gratitude as I realize that trickling beads of sweat have turned into streams rolling down my skin. Ah yes. My attention is on my senses enjoying the heat of the sauna. I am aware of the present moment.

I think about the mountain—that mountain I'm starting to have a love-hate relationship with. I do get it. There's no reason for me to worry and fear about climbing it. If a time comes when I do scale further up its side, then it will be okay. I will be able to handle it. I smile when I realize that I've left my vision with my Lord sitting on the ledge, alone. But we're good. He knows I've pretty much taken in what I can for today. Tomorrow we'll talk more.

Meanwhile, I look forward to *living in the present* becoming a way of life.

Chapter 25

Live Life

"You don't value life because you don't live life," the Lord says to me as I awake in the middle of the night, bored and unable to return to sleep.

He's got my attention. I have often, all throughout my life, acknowledged to him and to myself that I don't put as much value on my life as he does. If push came to shove and I were to find myself physically deteriorated, I would prefer death over living that way. This truth runs underneath my conscious, joyful self.

"Tell me more," I say to him.

"You barely use this life." I listen with surprise.

"You mostly just exist. You sit on a shelf watching what goes on around you. You occasionally jump off and into the play, but you never venture far, and before you know it, you're back in place on the shelf. Immobile, seemingly inanimate. If you lived more dynamically and more fully, you would appreciate the blood flowing through your veins."

"I see," I say. "It's like the saying that the benefit you get from something is based on what you're willing to put into it. It's measured and proportional."

"Yes, it is," he confirms.

This is a truth that's been slowly awakening in me—in my body as much as in my soul. It's time to live. To stop hiding where I can't be seen. To get off the shelf. It's time to put zeal and zest into life and living.

Time to be active: to walk and run and dance.

Time to connect: to experience new people and new places and new opportunities.

Time to fly: to rise above the limitations I've inflicted on myself. It's time to rise above the fears and above the weight that holds me to the ground.

"Okay, I hear you, Lord. So now what?"

"Now let's eat."

I get up and look for a late-night snack while he continues.

"Fuel yourself with that which will build your body, inspire your mind, and move your soul. Be mindful of what you take in. Some foods weigh you down and leave you only to sit on the shelf, gathering dust. Other foods are life-giving and will support you in all your endeavors."

I put down the chocolate Almond Joy and reach for an apple instead.

"I'll teach you," he says. "And then I'll show you what this baby can do!"

Chapter 26

Freedom

Freedom. I am reading an account of someone's life and his evolving view of the Lord. He says that he has a new perspective of God in his life, and because of that, he now feels freedom.

"That's the same thing I feel!" I say to the Lord. "Free." Of course, that carries a lot of possibilities for such a small, simple word. "What does that mean?"

I ponder my journey this past year. I am alone. Widowed. That is significant, yes; but even more significant is that I left the Christian ministry I was a part of for forty-five years. All my adult life.

I left a belief that I, being a woman, must have a male headship to oversee my life, my activities. A belief that I need someone outside of me and my Lord to confirm that what I am hearing and doing is the Lord's wisdom. I left a life of striving to disregard my wants—to sacrifice my desires, seeing them as unfit—and *obey the Lord* instead. I'm coming to understand that he never asked for that. My Lord and I are one. The more aware I become of this, the more I see we want the same thing.

"Is that what this freedom means?" I ask.

"You tell me."

"I suppose that's it," I say as I laugh. "For starters it means I don't have to go and ask you for answers, direction, and help as if you are outside of and apart from me. I have the answers within myself. I already know them because I know you." Kind of like a Dorothy in *The Wizard of Oz* experience. She had the shoes on her feet that would take her home all throughout the story. She didn't need to seek out the wizard to get home. The answer was always with her.

"Lord," I continue, "that means I don't have to try to do or be anything other than who I am. I don't have to do one single thing to be acceptable. I don't have to try to figure you out and try to please you."

"Good start," he says. "And that has come because you have been willing to look truth square in the face and not hide some lie in its place. The filters being removed from your perceptions will show you more and more of the truth—the truth about who I am and who you are. And in that truth, you will know me, us, you. That sparks freedom."

"It's freedom to be me," I say under my breath.

Chapter 27

Take Out the Trash

"**D**id you remember to take out the trash?" the Lord asks, though he knows I have not.

"The trash?" I respond. "Well, good morning to you, too, Lord. Why is the trash such a big deal that it's your first utterance of the day?" I look at the trash can in the corner of my room, full and ready to overflow if I try to toss one more thing into it. It seems harmless. No big deal in just letting it sit there.

"Clutter. It's about the clutter. You are trying to grow and not be slowed down by reluctance, by fear, or by lack of direction. But the clutter builds up around you and draws you aside. It's a distraction. It's time for some good cleaning, starting with trash removal," my Lord says to me. "That's the worst kind of clutter—leaving that which you have thrown away, leaving that residue, to yet take space in your life and fill the air around you."

I know I do need to clean my room. I do need to empty the trash, but I sense we're talking about much more than the physical here.

"Yes, it's also about your soul," he confirms. "Have you ever thrown something away, only to go back and pull it out of the trash again a day later?" We both know that I have. "You do that more than you realize. And you do it most often in your soul. You go back and look for what you already deemed was not useful to you, what does not serve you, what no longer works. You go back and pick it out of the trash heap in hopes it may have some resurrected benefit. Trust me. It doesn't," he says with finality.

He sits quietly while I ponder the words. I get it. The clutter I keep digging through disturbs my sleep. It's the lying in bed at night wondering about this, about that . . . about what I should have said differently, what signal I missed, whether I should go back and try to fix one situation or another, unraveling what I have already taken care of. It's endlessly digging through the trash bin.

I best get that bin emptied, remove it completely from the room.

"Let me help you with that," the Lord continues. "Let's burn it so that it doesn't remain a temptation to you."

That thought does make me flinch. It makes me realize that I like dumpster diving! Oh no, I didn't know that. It keeps me living in the past—the familiar, the comfortable— and keeps me from moving on down the road I'm standing on. This is part of that reluctance we've been discussing. Despite my good intentions and sincere commitment, I am still stuck, and this is why.

"Okay, Lord," I say, handing him a box of matches.

He hands them back to me.

"You do it. You set fire to the heap," he tells me. "I'll stand with you and make sure the flames don't touch you so that they cannot turn and consume you. I will watch over and cover you."

"Okay," I say. "After all, it is my trash."

I set the fire, and the flames warm me—not just the flesh of my skin but also the crevices of my soul. I sense that burning away the old and useless clutter makes room for something new. It's like prairie burning, when farmers burn their fields to the remove residue of old crops before they plant new ones.

It's not long before the blaze dims. The smoke rises, and behind it a clear blue sky emerges. Beauty from ashes.

It's not long before my lungs are cleared of the smoke I've inhaled. Before I'm breathing the breath of life.

It's not long before I rise and start once again to move forward, setting one foot in front of the other, eager to leave the past behind and give full attention to today. Undistracted. Alive.

Now I'm ready.

Chapter 28

Turn Around and Look

"Turn around and look at where you've come from. Look at where you've been," the Lord says to me early this morning.

I'm afraid to look back, afraid to see what is behind me. Afraid it will only point me to more of the same ahead. I do like and enjoy much of the past, but there's enough unpleasantness there to keep me from wanting to continue in it. Still, I turn and look.

"I don't see what I expected to see," I say. When I turn, I see a silver mist covering over what was my life up to this point. A shining, silver mist that makes everything seem so much softer, so much easier. "It's okay," I say to the Lord. "I'm not afraid of it now."

"Nor should you be," he says. "It's gone. It's behind you. You have feared that the darkness you felt in past times would—that it could—come up and overtake you. But it won't. You have grown beyond that, and what remains in your mind of the darkness is only in your mind. It's not alive. It cannot touch you now.

"When you play it over and over in your mind, it gains more darkness, more density, and more deceit. If you stop the imaginations and instead turn and look at what has been—straight on and without embellishment—it will release its hold on you. In place of dark fear, a luminous cloud will guide you into the brilliance of today's glow, today's promise.

"Today is not yesterday," he continues reassuringly. "Today you create anew."

"Thank you for that, Lord."

I close my eyes and let the words sink in. *I create today.* I draw in God's presence, letting it fill me. From this place, I go into today. I am in today and will live in today.

"I am present," I say aloud. "I live in this moment, this moment only, and it is good. It is uplifting. It is life."

Part Five

Pruning

Chapter 29

Bowels of Mercy

I've fallen into a deep sadness this afternoon, a feeling of loss, a mourning. I want to cry, yet the tears won't come. Rather, I feel numb. Simply numb. Void of feeling. Void of thought.

As I turn to the Lord, I have a vision of a tapeworm being pulled from me—from my bowels. Not from my heart, but from the bowels. *Bowels of mercy.* "What's that?" I ask.

"It's the hidden parasite that latched on to you when you were ever so young, so unaware. It took succor, drawing from you the mercy. Emptying your bowels of mercy, as it were. Suctioning off what was intended for another, that tapeworm robbed you of the gentleness that becomes mercy."

"That's a lot to take in. Can you break it down for me, Lord?"

"Sure. You have great love, a great capacity for love, within you, a great capacity to give love and to give mercy. But that life-form, the tapeworm, took root at your base and stole love and mercy from you. It siphoned the tenderness of mercy from you. That is what has left you to often fall into a state of numbness and to become dull to your senses.

"Today, I draw that worm out and away from you. Today you can begin once again to experience mercy, with love, with care. The reservoir will fill and overflow—out from you to wherever you direct it. You have life's flow stirring within you, flowing out from you. You feel it as a trickle now, but it shall grow."

That's so curious to me. I've been reading about love and suffering and caring and being vulnerable and giving to others. More specifically, I've been reading about feeling a sense of belonging, having close relationships and sharing lives. Having a connection reinforced by compassion, mercy, and love. It all sounds beautiful, but it is hard for me to connect. I mostly feel numb. I have always felt a bit of a hardness at my core, a hardness declaring I would not be vulnerable. I would not show myself. And so while I long to belong, I have resisted it. I don't reach out to others. I don't find connection. I mostly remain still and without motion.

"Lately, however," I say to the Lord, "my desire has been to come out from hiding and even to be vulnerable. The woods are not so welcoming as they once were since I've started to enjoy the beauty of the meadow. I'm not so afraid to be seen."

I fall into silence as I realize what has left me pierced and saddened. In the past few months, I've opened myself to someone. I became visible and let love flow out from me to this person. But that love isn't returned. It can't be returned to me. For reasons I understand, it can't be what I want.

"Lord, is this where mercy comes in? To continue to care and love without expecting anything in return? To have mercy even if I feel hurt or rejected?"

He nods his head. "Yes, and now you've grown to where you can be in that flow. That's what you're discovering. It may not feel good at the moment, but it is healing."

I consciously choose to sit and to heal. I am willing to let love's reservoir of mercy flow from me.

I continue to sit, still feeling numb. "Lord?"

"Rest now, my child. Rest for the labor that is at hand, for the work, for the walk, that is ahead. Feeling shall return. All shall be restored to you, and you will be whole in every way."

Chapter 30

Let Your Heart Break

In the heat of the sauna, I pick up on a conversation the Lord and I started earlier this morning. I've had time to think about it a bit, but I'm still not sure how to apply it. The Lord urged me to let my heart break and then said that together, we would heal it.

"Let my heart break? How do I do that, Lord?"

"Don't resist the feelings. Don't shut down when you start to feel hurt and disappointed. Don't suppress. That just turns your tenderness to a heart of stone."

I'm listening closely. That is what I tend to do. When negative feelings come up, the kind that break the heart, I shove them down. I refuse to feel them. I stiffen my jaw and numb my heart.

"Right," the Lord says. "That's what you usually do—until they build up to the point that you cannot push them down. Being compressed so tightly, they grow stronger, and then they erupt and throw you for a loop.

"Try this instead. Let feelings of hurt and pain go on through you. Let them pull you inside out. It feels dark. It seems hard, I know. But let yourself feel the pain until you reach the other side. You will come out stronger. You will grow richer, fuller, and truer to all that you really are."

"Start now? Do I start from here, where I am?" I ask, knowing already the answer is yes; knowing that it is certainly time. I've known it for a while but have been running from its shadow hovering over me, smothering me. It's time. There's no reason to wait.

I don't even need the Lord's response. I sit in silent meditation with trepidation and with a glimmer of hope.

Chapter 31

Be Still

"Looks like I've been AWOL for a while, Lord," I say as I look at the date on my last written conversation. A full month has passed. The truth is that we've still been doing quite a bit of talking . . . just not the kind I've felt like writing down. Our conversations have been more personal and unsettling. I'm not quite ready to think deeply about them yet. But today I feel the yearning to just chat.

"I like to chat with you," the Lord says. "You are a joy to me. You reach and you stretch to touch those things you do not know. I like it when you reach even beyond the low-hanging fruit to access something a bit higher, a bit more seemingly out of reach."

"Glad that you've noticed, Lord."

"So today let me give you something to challenge you," he says.

Now I've done it, I think. The phrase *brace for impact* comes to mind.

"Why do you go to the negative? I say I want to challenge you and you go right to a plane crash. What's up with that?" the Lord teases.

"Habit," I respond. No defense. No reason, for it has not even been reasoned out. Just a quick off-the-cuff remark. I seem to do that a lot.

"Well, moving on," he continues, "I want you to know that there are things you have desired, things you have hoped for, that have already come. That already are. You just do not yet see them because you are faced forward, looking to the future and missing what is now."

That takes my breath away. The profoundness of it.

"Today, look at only today," he says. "Forget tomorrow and what you're going to do or what will be. Let that go. Today, just be still and know. Be still."

"Today," I whisper. "So be it, Lord."

Chapter 32

Just Be

I feel playful today. Hopeful. So happy to step into the sauna.

"What's new today?" I ask the Lord. "What shall we talk about?"

"That depends on you," he replies. "What are you about? Still playing hide-and-seek? Looking for what you cannot find? Or content, enjoying who you are?"

"Ah, let's go with the latter," I say. "Content. Enjoying. Being. Experiencing the full range of me—who I now am."

Who I now am. Now. Being. It's startling to realize how much time I spend getting set up to be present. You know, getting this little thing done, that thing moved, clearing my way so I can sit in my special chair or step into the sauna where I can turn my attention inward, to me, to meditate. Busy, busy, busy . . . all so I can get still. What's up with that?

"It's your effort to control," I hear the Lord say. "You find doing is easier than being. You can control what you do, but to just *be*—well, there's nothing to control. It just is."

It just is. Simple and true.

I feel good today. I feel like this journey is producing results. Just like weeding and pruning a garden makes way for plant life to flourish, these past deep and cutting conversations have cleared my heart and sharpened my awareness. I'm learning. I'm becoming more present. I can stop and smell the roses. In my mind's eye I can even prune and shape them. I can nourish and water them. I can see them, touch them, smell and even taste them. I can be pricked by their thorns, feel the pain and not back away.

Chapter 33

No Do-Overs

I get the sauna heat up really hot, really steaming; and then I cry out to the Lord. I think about David and feel such regret, such sadness that I lost him, that he is gone. It's strange how memories and regrets come when I least expect them. Like today. It's been two years since David passed away. I'm going about my normal routine, and I think I'm beyond grief. Then some emotion stirs. Some faint memory sharpens, and I'm emotionally pulled to an earlier time.

As I let go, my tears cleanse and release what is pent up inside. I feel thankful and happy that in the last months, maybe the last few years of our life together, I finally got my priorities right.

I am thankful for the time I left work early or rearranged my schedule to be with David, even to sit and do nothing. At the same time, I feel remorse that I didn't do this more often. I'm sorry that it took a series of strokes and desperation to learn what was important. I wish I would have experienced better priorities all throughout our life together, when circumstances were good, when there was no need to do so, when my action could have come simply from a heart of love and appreciation.

As tears continue down my cheeks, I see myself lying on a stone bed carved out in a cave. The Lord comes in, sits down, and lifts my head into his lap as I cry. I know it's okay. In his gentle care, I know that *I* am okay.

"Lord," I confess, "the regret I feel is not just that I wasn't present with David throughout our marriage. It's also that I didn't really know me as well as I do now. I didn't know me well enough to comfortably sit and be silent with me. It isn't just about David. It's about me."

I lived my whole life conforming to what I thought was expected of me. I spent so much time and attention on my job rather than tending to relationships because I thought that was what I was supposed to do. I was conscientious. I was responsible. So dependable. My employers could always count on me.

Further, I buried my wants and needs as being unimportant. I was proud of being so strong. Being the one everyone could depend on. But in the end, I came to see that this was not what mattered most. I only began to see that as I set all else aside and sat with David while he lay dying. Next to him was where I wanted to be.

"You're only now coming to understand that, aren't you?" the Lord says. "Speak it aloud now. What would you say to your younger self?"

I think about how my life priorities were mixed up. Deeper than that, I let things that hurt or trouble me pass by as unimportant—as if I was unimportant. I set David above me in our relationship rather than standing alongside him as an equal. I think about how I used distractions—such as my job—to avoid facing this.

What I would say now is this:

"Silence, avoidance, busyness—it's all just as detrimental as fighting, yelling, and cutting with words. It yields no fruit, and one day you will look back and wish you could have a do-over, but you can't.

"You will wish you had lived your life as yourself and not buried your identity under some false obligation to what you're supposed to do, who you're supposed to be. One day, when you are willing to seriously face the truth, you will find yourself excavating the ground on which you have lived. You will find yourself looking for you, for a remnant of the true you that was left behind and hidden so that you could be more acceptable, more normal, more like what you thought people wanted.

"The truth is, as you will find, your carefully fashioned false self did not provide anything you hoped it would. Regardless of what you did, people still found you unacceptable by their standards and expectations. You didn't fit in as you desired. You weren't normal. As if anyone knows what normal is!

"Your fulfillment can only come in being truly you, living from your very core, from your centered oneness with God. In the end, that is the only you who can love, who can give anything of life to your mate, your family, your friends, to the world. That is who can add to their well-being. And that truth will fulfill you," I finish, surprised at the depth of my words.

"Well said," the Lord whispers as he strokes my hair.

"And the truth is, Lord, this person I am now, and am growing into being, is someone I know David would have appreciated even more than the version of me he knew. I wish I had been able to give this true self to him."

Chapter 34

Aerate the Soul

"Aerate the soul." That's what I hear this morning as I meditate in the sauna. Specifically, the Lord tells me that meditating is like aerating the soul. What a beautiful image! Wonderful thought! Now, what does that mean?

I'm taken to words from another conversation the Lord and I had together: *"I get the sense that my journey into meditation and learning to be still has much to do with letting nature unfold in its time. My life will unfold when my soul and spirit—like the earth and the atmosphere—have been prepped and call it forth."*

I believe that this aerating is prepping my soul and spirit.

"Indeed, it is," the Lord says. "It's breaking up the density of thought that weighs you down day after day. The continual conjuring, thinking, imagining, planning—it is so dense that you cannot move forward. As you meditate, as you become still and sit without agenda, you let the spirit move and break up the hardness—the weight—that holds you down."

"It brings me into peace," I suggest.

"It lets peace emanate; it flows from you."

"So that is aerating the soul," I mumble quietly, in soft breath tones. I know there is more to consider, to meditate on, and in time it will become clear. But for now, I'm satisfied. My soul is calmed. My heart content.

Chapter 35

Fly Like an Eagle—Really?

"Lord? It's snowing and cold outside. I feel lost and alone inside. What do I do?" I ask as I look out my window. A thick layer of white blankets the earth.

"Fly, my child," my Lord responds. "Lift your head, raise your arms, close your eyes, and let your spirit soar. Let it soar above what you can see. Soar above the cold. Open your eyes and look about, you will see the cold is only temporary. The fire within you, the warmth, never fades away and is never overtaken by anything outside of you.

"You, my child, must learn to live in the spirit, in the warmth of my love and my care, rather than in what you see. You are prone to watch and give attention to the world of circumstances, of people acting and reacting to or ignoring you. You look for signs to determine how you should act and react. This brings you to immobility and to coldness. You freeze in place. Void of life. It is this way of living that invites the snow to cover the embers of love in your heart, in your soul."

"Well, I'd say that about sums it up, Lord."

I am saddened to think about how quickly I seem to turn from the Lord and love and warmth, to become engulfed in a snowstorm of circumstances, doubt, and confusion. So quickly it happens.

"Not so quickly," the Lord interrupts. "Not really. You court it. You tire of the warmth, and you go looking for something else, something to stir emotion within you. Be it good or bad emotion, you want only for something to stir life within, something to pull you out of numbness."

Do I really go out looking for what will make me suffer? Can that be? I'm in disbelief. It's as though I've connected this hurting and searching—feeling unsettled—with feeling I'm alive and having worth. If I'm experiencing joy and peace and calm—with no need to strive and hustle—then I'm not satisfied.

"Yes. Consider what that says about you," the Lord encourages me.

I take a stab at a response. "It is obvious I don't yet believe in who I am and my value, my worth, my gift to this earth."

Actually, I have an inkling of it, but I shy away from it. Who am I to be so bold? What have I to give? I'm more apt to fall in line with the masses and create a life of suffering, lacking fulfillment, being incomplete, always questioning. I recall a vision someone once had for me: He saw me as an eagle soaring in the sky high above the earth, as described in the Bible in Isaiah 40:31. "*They who wait on the* LORD *. . . shall mount up with wings like eagles; they shall run and not be weary; they shall walk and not faint.*" That was how he saw me, not as a chicken pecking on the ground.

My reaction? *I don't want to be an eagle flying alone in the sky. I'd rather peck the ground with all the other chickens.* Silly girl. Sad girl. Unfulfilled girl.

"So, Lord, looks like it's time for me to soar like an eagle— like a majestic, glorious, and bold eagle in full flight high in the heavens. Looks like it's time for me to break from the snow-covered minutia and fulfill my purpose. Is that what I'm hearing?"

"Yes, my child. That's what you're hearing. It's time."

"I can do that," I answer as I begin to shake the cold from my limbs and to raise my hands upward. I lift my head and stare squarely at the sunrays pouring through the window. I draw warmth to my insides and let it melt what held me in a frozen state. No longer stiff, I lift my body onto the tip of my toes to prepare for takeoff.

Part Six

Becoming

Chapter 36

Numbness

Sitting in the sauna today I explore my fears. What am I afraid of? I am afraid of *not* feeling numb. I'm afraid of having desire, of feeling desire. Afraid of the consequences if that which I desire is not attainable. Afraid that I will want and long for something that cannot be. So instead, I grow numb. Numb and safe from unrequited desire.

"Yes, you have made Numbness your protector," the Lord says.

"I know," I respond. "The first time Numbness showed up, he made me feel better. Took the edge off some of the pain, the insecurity."

"And soon you and Numbness were the best of buddies."

"Yes, we became very close. I learned to depend on him and always, always acquiesce to his presence, relieving myself of the need to be present. I learned to substitute his nothingness—his distractions—for my own self, my own truth."

"And eventually even you forgot what it was you desired. You buried it and forgot."

"But now it's making itself known once again," I report,

opening the door to discuss it with my Lord. "I may need a little help with that."

"Yes. Now you're feeling secure enough to let it be seen. You have taken a step away from Numbness and have begun to explore what lies within you, still and unassuming. Shelved and hidden away.

"Take your time and keep recovering what it is. It's your desire, and it's precious. You can voice it now and stand present, even in the face of fear."

"I sense that to be true, Lord. And even if I do fear that I will be rejected, that I will fail to experience what I desire, that it is out of reach, I know that I must be firm and stretch to reach for it nonetheless. I can touch it. It's mine. It's worth the risk, the struggle. It's time to own it, in presence and in fullness."

"Yes, it is. Just like when a butterfly knows it's time to wrestle free from its cocoon. You have struggled. You have danced with fear and with truth. You have given all you knew to give and then even more.

"Yes, wrestle free and feel the wind carry you out of your shell, my child. It is strong enough to do that, and it is time."

Chapter 37

Let's Talk About Love

"**G**ood morning, Lord."

"Good morning. Let go of the weight on your shoulders. You look tired, and you look heavyhearted."

"I am, Lord. I'm tired and I'm somewhat sad. Though I'm happy to say I've not felt sadness like this for a long time. I've been running with joy in the sunshine and feeling really good. Learning so much. Learning of you and feeling your love for me and learning to love those around me. At the same time, it's not easy, is it? I feel a bit drained."

"Let me share this with you about love. It is not something you can put into a box to give to someone. Once you box it up, you have set it apart—you've set it away from you. It is no longer part of you, and so it is no longer love. Love is only shared in relationship to someone or something else."

I add to the conversation. "And in relationship you are not in control of the other person's response. Sometimes you're not even in control of yourself—or so it seems. Love is not just up to you. It's what is shared between the persons."

"That's a good start," the Lord tells me, "but go beyond that. It does not end with what you share. It lives beyond the interaction, beyond what you can touch, beyond what you can control. True love has nothing to do with the other person; and at the same time, it has everything to do with the other person. Think about that for a while."

"I'll have to think about that for a really long while," I respond. Admittedly, the concept is beyond my grasp at the moment.

"It's okay. You've got lots of time. Go ahead and give it all the time and space you need, but do consider it. I'll be around when you want to talk further."

"Fair enough, Lord. Fair enough."

Chapter 38

To Receive Love

"Lord," I say as I start around the small lake where I've come to walk. "I'm willing to receive love, to be open to a soul mate to share the rest of my life with." It's the middle of a conversation we've been having. After David passed away, I decided I would not remarry. David and I had worked through our difficulties and struggles together and had come through with a solid, good marriage. Why would I want to go through all of that again? Relationships are not easy. Why would I want to risk following a good one with a relationship that might be less than what I had with David? Maybe I'd want to compare the new man in my life to David. Then I'd miss David even more.

I walk with that thought circling in my head. Relationships are a risk. My mind tells me I had a good marriage and I should leave it at that. My heart is suggesting otherwise, suggesting that some relationships are worth the risk. Suggesting, asking, that I open my heart to explore the possibility.

I take a deep breath and pause. I think I do want someone. I don't like waking up alone. I want a warm body to snuggle with, to laugh with and to dream with. Someone to hold me.

Someone to love me. What really troubles me is that there is someone I've begun to spend time with, someone who is drawing that desire out in me. My heart has already started warming up to him, but I fear the thought of such a relationship. I long for it, but then my mind says no. I turn and run.

As I continue my walk, I think about what I have to do to open up. How do I need to change? What would be required of me? How do I open my heart?

The Lord responds. "Just be willing to give the same thing you seek. Be willing to love without looking for return. Love simply because it flows from you. Don't restrain it. Be willing to look at and admire the man. See him in his truth and beauty. Be willing to touch him, to caress him and let him know how you feel about him. Be vulnerable and unafraid."

I think on this. Maybe I can be that. A big maybe.

"And what are you willing to give up for this relationship?" the Lord asks. "Let's talk about that."

"Huh?" I mumble.

Then an alluring song begins to play in my head. In my youth I thought it was strange how Simon and Garfunkel greeted darkness with musicality. Suddenly, the meaning of their lyrics becomes crystal clear.

Darkness. Darkness and sounds of Silence. They are who I run to now to hold me and caress me and soothe my hurts. Am I willing to trade them for a live body, for someone in the flesh? Ah. I must give up my current lovers, Darkness and Silence.

"Yes," the Lord says. "As long as you have them—Darkness and Silence—waiting in the wings, ready to run to, you will not let go and give yourself fully to another."

I want to say yes, that I will give them up, but I know it is not that easy, and I won't answer glibly as though it were. "I need your help for that, Lord. Show me how."

"I will," he says. "I will."

* * *

Once I return home, I take a seat at my window. I'm comforted by a sobering yet welcoming scene. Winter is here. The trees lay bare, and snow is beginning to settle on their limbs, limbs that reach out but can find no warmth. Somewhat like me, reaching, just a little bit, but finding no warmth. Winter. It's a time to rest, a time to lie low. Soon the trees will bud once again—a gentle reminder that life goes on. Life goes on in the earth. Life goes on inside me. But today, I take in the stillness of winter.

I quiet my mind. I invite the Lord to show me more about this new lesson. I am afraid to let go of Darkness and Silence. They're familiar companions. Oh how I feel safe and secure cuddled up and nestled in their arms.

In a vision the Lord takes me into a dense forest—into total darkness and total silence. I give a low sigh. *Ah, here I am.*

Do I feel good? Warmed? Safe? Hell no! I'm scared. I'm alone in the dark in a place I don't know. I don't like it.

"But that's what Darkness and Silence are, my dear," the Lord begins to explain. He unveils for me the quiet, endless lovers I have chosen instead of a real man made of flesh.

"You have attributed traits to these lovers that are not there. Darkness and Silence have nothing. They do not reach out to you to hold you. They do not warm you with their touch. They just sit there, impersonal and overbearing. You have imagined them to be a womb of security and unending love. That's all a fabrication of your mind."

"I feel so foolish. It really is an empty place, isn't it?" I say, speaking more to myself than to the Lord. Darkness. Silence. I've fooled myself.

Upon this realization, the dark embrace I have so treasured turns cold. There's no longer an allure. It is nothing I've longed for.

"Now we can begin," the Lord says. "Now we can begin to pull from you that which is in your heart, that which will give you strength to walk out of that forest—*to step away from the woods*," he says with a wink. "That false illusion is broken."

"Yes, it is, Lord. So be it," I answer as a tear slips down my cheek.

Chapter 39

From the Core of Your Being

"Lord, I love you. I love you because you love me. I wouldn't even think to love, to know you, had you not originated it," I say as I take a moment to spend with my Lord God. I am aware that sometimes I just don't appreciate him and his love enough. I fall short in the gratitude department.

"You make me smile," he responds. "You still think that loving, giving, knowing . . . that everything you do is an episodic event. That you take a moment to love, to spend time with me, when in reality, you are with me all the time. Your love is constant in the universe. It doesn't start and stop. It's only your conscious awareness that starts and stops it."

"Sounds like then I'm loving even when I don't know it. It just exudes from me," I say, feeling rather proud of my ever-loving little self. But then the opposite occurs to me as well. "And then maybe I'm hating even when I don't know it." That does not evoke pride in me. It brings confusion. Then how do I know what I'm sending out? Is there a switch I flip one way or the other? Is it based on my conscious thoughts? What's the deal?

"It comes from the core of your being," the Lord says. "It

comes from what you identify with, not from your actions, not even from your thinking. It's deeper than that. What you do adds to it, strengthens or weakens it, but it is from a deeper place than you have recognized within yourself. Love comes from intimacy with me within you."

I instantly recognize that as truth. I don't know what it means, how to rationalize it or figure it out, but I know it's true. It resonates with me in my spirit.

"Lord, I perceive this lesson as something to let seep into my soul, to simply receive and then let be. I don't need to understand the mechanics of it."

"Yes. Don't labor over it. Let it permeate you, and you will come to know more fully. That knowing will bypass your mind and your thinking, and you will come to understand what it is to be love. Then being love, you will give it without thought, without restraint, without works, without trying. It will simply be in you and come from you even as it is with me."

Now it's my turn to smile. "Yes, Lord. I am love."

Chapter 40

Jump into the Deep End

"Hey, Lord, you remember my new quest I said I would pursue? To love unconditionally? To be like you? To give love without expectation, without judging, without looking for it in return? I've been working on that. I've failed."

"That's okay," he answers. "You've got a bit of a learning curve to this. I'm encouraged with your progress."

Yes, it's true. I've been inspired. I sensed a glimpse of God's unconditional, ever-giving, nonending love, and the desire grew within me to love the same way.

I knew it could be a little hard, so I chose someone to try it out on. At first it was going well. I could just love without any hesitation and without worrying about how he would respond to me. But then I began to feel let down. Like I was just shooting love off into some dark hole where it disappeared. I was not feeling so fulfilled by being able to give this love (I know—expectations), and now here I am.

"I am encouraged with you," the Lord continues, bringing my attention back to him. "You jumped into the deep end of the pool. I remember a time when you would never do that, but now you have. You're not quite able to swim there yet, but you are willing. You are open to it, and that is a beautiful thing."

I reflect on this. When I was a child, my parents put me in swimming lessons. Over time I did fairly well. I learned to dog paddle well enough to keep myself out of trouble. I could float—I just couldn't hold my breath to keep my head under water all that long. Eventually I could make it across the pool without touching the bottom, all the while knowing that if I needed to stand up and touch it, I could. I was in the shallow end.

For graduation we were required to jump off the diving board into the deep end of the pool and swim (or dog-paddle or float) to the side of the pool. Not a long distance. Much shorter than what I had been practicing in the shallow end. But alas, it was my turn to jump, and I would not. That water was way over my head, and I was not going in. I stood motionless and shook my head no. I failed the class.

My parents enrolled me again the next summer. Again, I did well. I was able to do everything the instructor taught until graduation day. Then once again I refused to jump into the deep end. Isn't God funny to remind me of that?

Returning to our conversation, I respond, "It feels kind of beautiful, too, Lord. So where do I go from here?"

"Let's edge our way down the side of the pool back to the shallow end. Get you back into a comfort zone for a moment where you can practice some more."

As I continue in the vision, we move along the side of the pool, holding on to the edge until I can safely let go and jump into the middle, proudly standing on my own two feet.

"Now that you're feeling safe again, let's talk," he says.

I nod my head, listening intently.

"You have been working hard on giving unconditional love. That concept is faulty. It cannot bring you to what you seek. When you *give*, you are drawing from what you have. You will run out, as you've seen."

That's true. I evidently didn't have very much stored up inside to give.

"I say to you to *be* love. *Be* unconditional love. What you have done is noteworthy, but better is to simply *be*. Be love and know that it is without expectation. When you can be, you don't even need to give thought to how much you're giving without return. There is no scorecard. It is love. You are love, as I am love. There are no conditions set to guide who gets it, when they can have it, and why it's going to them.

"Rather, you are simply being you. The true, full you who is one with me and fulfilled with me. There is no separation between us. You are loved, and you are love."

"Back to the drawing board," I respond. "I so missed that key bit. I see that if I am picking who to give love to (and therefore who not to give it to), it's not so unconditional as I thought. I'm hearing that with the idea of me *giving* love, I draw from what I think I have, and that is limited."

"Yes. Still, you put what you did understand into motion. You picked your feet up off the floor and began to kick and to move through the water, propelled by more than having your feet on solid ground. It's a process. So no, you have not failed. You are in the process of becoming aware of what you are. You are becoming what is you—love. Unconditional, unmeasurable love."

"And soon, I'll jump off that diving board into the deep waters and not even notice where I am, right?"

"Soon, you'll be swimming in those waters without even realizing that you entered them," he counters with a smile.

I smile too.

Chapter 41

They're Just Like Me

January 1. A new day, a new year. Yet I really don't see much that is different from yesterday or from the year just ended. Why would there be? The changing from one year to the next is only a numerical designation, not an actual change in nature. It is not noted in the universe. Still, it is a landmark that calls many of us to pause from everyday activity, from business as usual, to review our lives and to plan for the future. I, thankfully, have a cocreator in that planning.

"Lord," I say and then pause, not knowing what to ask, what to comment, where to go with this. I only know a longing to talk with him and to hear his guiding voice. I sit in silence and in my vision find myself seated with him on that small ledge up on the mountain where we have often engaged. Looking at people passing on the well-marked trail below, I'm tempted to toss pebbles at them to get their attention, to disrupt their aimless, uneventful wandering.

"You want to walk with them awhile?" the Lord asks. "Let's do that."

Suddenly I find myself on the trail, walking in step with a

handful of others. "Good morning. Isn't it a beautiful day?" I say in greeting to them.

"Good morning," a few softly reply. Another grunts an acknowledgment and one more nods her head. Not a talkative bunch, I gather. I fall into line with their pace and walk in silence. They're all absorbed in their own thoughts, in their plans for when they'll arrive at their destination.

Me? I have no plans. I don't even know where I'm walking to!

"What's the story here, Lord?" I ask. "They're like me, aren't they? Just trying to get to some other place, trying to create a plan—a plan that can occupy their minds and give them a sense of purpose. Trying to feel worthy of the blood flowing through their bodies. Trying to appreciate the gift of life. Looking for answers to the questions they don't know to ask."

"Yes, they are. Just like you, they've walked a well-laid-out trail carved by others. Those others—those who blazed the trails—did so in newness and in strength, in awareness and appreciation for their surroundings. They were conscious of the immediacy of their travel and embraced it. They observed nature and worked harmoniously with it to make the best path. As they moved through the forests, I whispered to them through the trees. I gave them direction. Boulders and stones created detours to guide them from one direction to another that could be traveled more safely. These sojourners were alive unto all creation. They were alive unto me and intently attuned to my voice. Their senses were sharp. Together we created the path, passing from destination to destination, growing and learning the process. Just as I do with you."

"And I appreciate that," I say.

"But now, those who follow on the trails made by others miss out on discovery. They look to bypass pain and unknowing. They want it all laid out, danger-free, risk-free. They want to mindlessly walk along and know exactly where the path will take them. Their senses grow weak for lack of use. They have invested nothing in the walk. They have nothing invested in their lives, really. They're merely putting in their time and pushing on to tomorrow where they suppose something new will pop up and they will know they have arrived at their destination.

"In this, they lose sensitivity to my voice. They lose awe of creation. They do not see its beauty nor appreciate that I have made it for them. They do not see what I have made in them. They are not aware that I dwell in them, that we walk together where they walk. They don't know that we have already arrived, that our destiny is already here.

"They catch only brief glimpses of life's reality. And when they do, they make a monument at that place of awareness so they can show it to the multitude of others who follow. They mark the place so they can save others from the ambiguity and the pain of forging their own routes. Their desire to help others is good, yet it is misguided. They don't consider that others have the same spirit, the same creation, and me walking with them to carve their own unique paths."

I quietly reflect on his words. Finally, I say, "That's why we left the path and you took me up the mountainside, Lord. I'm a pioneer, not a follower. You love me that much."

We take a moment to sit on a boulder to the side of the road. I breathe deeply. Creation. It fills my senses—its gracious beauty, its gentle sound, the fresh fragrance I inhale. A wayward leaf blows across my lap, and I bring it to my lips to touch it and awaken the last of my senses to the moment. I taste it. It is oddly satisfying, beyond words of description.

I sit in silence with my Lord. The need to create a plan and a vision for the future fades. I am complete. Whether on this flat, easy trail or clinging to the face of a mountain, I am content.

The taste of nature lingers with me. The taste of life, of love, of faith—it's sufficient. I will continue to journey beyond this benchmark as I turn the calendar page from one year to the next.

Conclusion

It's been a year since my last entry in these conversations with God. I've continued to talk with him, of course, but I haven't been as compelled to write down our exchanges. Perhaps it's because the upheaval in my life began to settle. I was finding my way, little by little, learning to step away from the woods and to dance in open meadows. I didn't know what my future would bring, but I had confidence I would be okay.

Or perhaps I stopped writing the conversations because I moved from my Indiana home. I no longer had access to the dry sauna, the treadmill, and the window chair with a view of the red maple tree. My routine changed when the family sold their home and we all moved to the Pacific Northwest.

I can see very clearly that my year of these intimate conversations prepared my soul for a new season of life. I have come through breaking up old ground, tilling new ground, planting, pruning, and tending to my heart and to my soul. In retrospect, I can see that what I did next was possible because of the attention I gave to my soul's garden during this year.

What did I do next?

I made a pilgrimage. I walked the Camino de Santiago (the Way of St. James).

The Camino is a 483-mile pilgrimage trail across northern Spain. Pilgrims have been walking it for over one thousand years—ever since the ninth century, when the remains of St. James, one of the apostles of Jesus, were discovered and enshrined in a cathedral in Santiago de Compostela. In 2019 almost 350,000 pilgrims were recorded to have walked to the Cathedral. I was one of them.

When I set out on this walk at age sixty-four, I wasn't thinking about it in terms of pilgrimage. I thought it would be a good opportunity to figure out what to do with my next thirty years. I thought it would be a good mental activity. I would be able to think, free of distractions, and plot out the rest of my life.

That's not what I found.

Rather, the pilgrimage broke me wide open. The experience continued what these conversations with God started. It connected me even more deeply with my soul, with the truth of who I am. It pierced the crusted earth that had formed a shell over me. Once I returned home I began to stand tall, assured in my being, no longer content to hunker down and sit just below the surface. By the time I returned home I knew myself better. I stepped out of numbness, rediscovered my purpose, and found the courage to live life fully.

You can read my pilgrimage story in detail in *Keep Walking, Your Heart Will Catch Up: A Camino de Santiago Journey.*

Notes

Epigraph:

1   Richard Rohr, "Order, Disorder, Reorder," Center for Action and Contemplation, July 14, 2017, https://cac.org/daily-meditations/order-disorder-reorder-2017-07-14/.

Preface:

1 Richard Rohr, *The Wisdom Pattern: Order, Disorder, Reorder* (Cincinnati, OH: Franciscan Media, 2020).

Chapter 6

A Few Good Men, directed by Rob Reiner, written by Aaron Sorkin, starring Jack Nicholson (Culver City, CA: Columbia Pictures, 1992), DVD, 2:06:29-2:06:50.

Acknowledgments

Bringing a book from an idea to actual publication is a big process. Sometimes challenging and a bit overwhelming, and other times fully energizing and exciting. I am so happy I did not make the journey alone. I had a lot of help. A lot. I truly appreciate the support and contributions from several people.

Thank you to my editor, Whitney Bak from The Editorial Department. Your edits and questions taught me so much about writing and providing context for my readers. This book has a warmer feel and a smoother flow because of your guidance and expertise. You showed me what a difference a good editor can make!

I'm indebted to a number of people who read the earliest versions of the manuscript and gave me such valuable feedback and insight on its potential, plus the courage to continue working on it. Thank you to Linda Bond, Juanita Stanley Holman, Barbara Kelly, Darla Kroesen, Katharyn Muniz, Amy Prevedel, and AnaMaria Ruiz.

Thank you to Kathleen Horstmeyer who walked with me through all the experiences of these conversations and continues to support and encourage my aspirations and adventures. And, thank you to AnaMaria Ruiz who shows me what it is to be a friend and to believe and to take action.

I appreciate the coaches and leaders who have inspired and encouraged me to own my voice and step into my calling as an author and speaker. Thank you to Geoffrey Berwind for coaching me in storytelling and having the courage to live my purpose, and to Steve Harrison, Jack Canfield and Patty Aubrey for the Mastermind Retreat which moved me and inspired me to kick into high gear.

Finally, I am thankful to have Raymond Corder in my life to believe in me and push me to believe in myself. You came into my life just when I needed you. Thank you, Ray.

About the Author

Cathay Reta is on a mission to help people who struggle to find or recover their passion, to know their purpose and to live fully. It's something she knows about because a few years ago life shook her foundation enough that she started to question everything she had believed. Listening to her inner voice, she took a walk—a long walk—on the Camino de Santiago (the Way of St. James), a 483-mile pilgrimage trail across northern Spain. Traveling alone, she got to know herself again and to fall in love with that self she rediscovered. On the Camino she also found the courage to pursue her dream of being an author and speaker.

Cathay has a diverse background with a B.A. degree in music; a lifetime of co-ministry with her late husband David; and a fifty-year career in adult literacy, developing and conducting training for local, statewide (California), and national organizations—most often with public libraries.

Cathay's greatest passion is turning life's experiences and observations into relatable lessons for others. Her mantra is:

You can do anything.
You are unstoppable.
You are amazing!
Now live it!

* * *

Did you like the book? If so, please leave a review on Amazon. It helps to get word out about it and to get it into the hands of more readers.

Connect with Cathay

Subscribe to her blog, invite her to speak to your group, or send a message via her website: www.cathayreta.com

www.ingramcontent.com/pod-product-compliance
Lightning Source LLC
Chambersburg PA
CBHW071328150726
17997CB00002B/630